Orville Bright

Elementary English

Orville Bright

Elementary English

ISBN/EAN: 9783337119492

Printed in Europe, USA, Canada, Australia, Japan

Cover: Foto ©Paul-Georg Meister /pixelio.de

More available books at **www.hansebooks.com**

ELEMENTARY ENGLISH

BY

ROBERT C. METCALF
Supervisor of Schools, Boston, Mass.

AND

ORVILLE T. BRIGHT
Superintendent of Schools, Cook County, Ill.

NEW YORK ∴ CINCINNATI ∴ CHICAGO
AMERICAN BOOK COMPANY

PREFACE.

This book is designed to supply or to suggest material for a three years' course in elementary language work, and to form a fitting introduction to Metcalf's *English Grammar*.

Since most of the language teaching in the schools should be based upon the regular work of the classroom, an effort has been made to show how lessons in reading, geography, history, and, above all, nature study, may be made to contribute to the language training of pupils. Each lesson is intended to be a suggestion of other similar lessons, which can be prepared readily by the teacher. Natural history affords a whole storehouse of suitable subjects, which is opened up by such lessons as those on "Cherry Buds," "The Spider," "The Frog," "The Coral," and "The Sponge." The possibilities of geography are shown by the lessons on "Warm Countries," "Cold Countries," "Our Own Country," and "Neighborhood Study." History furnishes abundant material, as shown in the historical studies preparatory to letter-writing and formal composition.

By means of pictures and suggested stories, many lessons have been made for the purpose of training the imagination, and also of increasing the power of the children to express their thoughts in good English. Such lessons may be multiplied to any extent deemed necessary by the teacher. In connection with these lessons, the best fables, fairy tales, and folk-stories should be read by the children, and then the stories should be retold by them in their own words.

Many simple poems are given to be read and committed to memory, and occasionally to be studied, for the purpose of interesting the children in poetic forms, thus preparing the way for a more extended study of poetic literature in the higher grades of the schools.

The mechanism of composition has not been neglected. The chapter on letter-writing gives all needed information concerning capital letters, punctuation, and forms; while great care has been taken to indicate how pupils may be prepared for writing compositions by previous study, note taking, and oral class work.

The last chapter in the book is devoted to grammar. In the development of the language lessons in the preceding pages, no attempt has been made to introduce this subject, except when essential to the use of good English. So many children leave school, however, before completing the grammar school course, that it was not deemed wise to omit the subject entirely. These lessons have been made simple. They include only the easier constructions in English, and the classifications of words into parts of speech.

The selections from Holmes, Longfellow, Lowell, Whittier, and the Cary sisters, which appear in the various language exercises, are used by permission of and arrangement with Messrs. Houghton, Mifflin & Company. Acknowledgment is due also to Messrs. D. Appleton & Company for permission to use several selections from the copyright works of William Cullen Bryant. For convenience of reference, a full list of the publications containing the works of the authors mentioned above may be found on page 200.

The "Notes" found at the close of many of the lessons call the attention of teachers to several other poems, which it is hoped they will find time to read with their pupils.

CHAPTER I.

LESSON I.

SENTENCES — STATEMENTS.

(Oral and then Written.)

See if you can find out what the picture tells.
1. What has the lady been doing? What interrupted her?
2. Is the child the lady's daughter? Is she a beggar? What do you think she is trying to do?
3. Does the lady want her matches? What is the lady asking the girl? Can you tell the girl's sad story?

A group of words which expresses a complete thought is a sentence.

Now ask the questions above, and, as your teacher or classmates answer them, tell whether they use complete sentences or only parts of sentences.

SENTENCES — QUESTIONS.

A sentence that tells something is a statement.

Write four statements.

With what kind of letter have you begun each sentence?
What mark have you placed after each statement?

Every statement is a sentence.
Every written sentence should begin with a capital.
Every written statement should end with a period.

LESSON II.

SENTENCES — QUESTIONS.

(Oral and then Written.)

Before you ask a question, you must think. A group of words which is used in asking a question is a sentence, because it expresses a thought.

See if you can learn the story which the picture tells by asking questions of your teacher.

1. Ask what the old man has been doing. Ask some question about his rake and his wheelbarrow. Also, find out, if you can, for what he uses the basket.

HOW TO WRITE NAMES. 7

2. Ask why the little birds are so tame.
3. Ask about anything else you would like to know.
4. Ask your teacher to tell or read you some story about a tame bird.

Number your questions, and see how many good ones you can ask. How many sentences have you used in asking questions about the picture?

What kind of letter begins each question? Make a rule about this.

Change your questions to statements. What two kinds of sentences can you name?

Exercise.

Which of the following sentences are statements? Which are questions? What mark follows the statements? What mark follows the questions?

1. Fido is a good dog.
2. Did you see him run?
3. Does he trouble the kitten?
4. Some dogs bark at cats.

Every written question should begin with a capital.
Every written question should end with a question mark.

LESSON III.

HOW TO WRITE NAMES.

Dictation Exercise.

Study the following sentences so that you can write them correctly: —

1. Does Anna May Brown live in Boston?
2. James Henry Norton went to New York.
3. Do you know George Lee Davis?
4. Chicago is in Illinois.
5. Do you live in West Virginia?

Oral Exercise.

Answer the following questions with oral statements: —

How many names are there in the first sentence? The first name is the name of what? The second is the name of what? How many words are there in each name?

Tell the names in the second sentence.

How many words are in the name in the third sentence? How many names are there in the fourth sentence? in the fifth? Of what are they names?

How many capitals did you use in the first sentence? in the second? the third? the fourth? the fifth? Why?

How many periods did you use? Why?

How many question marks? Why?

Every word in the special name of a person or place should begin with a capital.[1]

LESSON IV.

GIVEN NAMES AND FAMILY NAMES.

A father's name is *James Johnson.* The name of one son is *Henry Johnson*, and of the other, *Charles Louis Johnson.* The daughter's name is *Alice Maud Johnson.*

The name which is the same for all the members of the family is called the **family name,** or **surname.**

The name which is given to a boy or girl is called the **given name.**

Exercise.

Answer in statements the following questions: —

What word is the same in all the names above? What is the given name of each person mentioned? What is the family name? What is your surname? your given name? your father's given name?

[1] See note 1, page 45.

INITIALS.

How do people come by their surnames? How do they come by their given names? Why are they called *given* names?

Carefully write the names of ten persons whom you know.

LESSON V.

INITIALS.

Many people write only one word of their given names. They sometimes write one name and a letter to stand for the other, or one letter for each given name. A man may write his name *Charles Henry Black*, *Charles H. Black*, or *C. H. Black.*

The first letter of a word is called an **initial**. When the initial stands alone, it should be followed by a period.

Exercise I.

Write the following names when pronounced by your teacher : —

John R. Davis.	Miss M. A. Tanner.
Mary E. Ray.	R. B. Stone.
L. A. Freeman.	George B. Putnam.

Exercise 2.

Write from your book the following names with one initial and then with two —

Arthur Allen Morse.	Oliver Wendell Holmes.
Elizabeth Cady Stanton.	Henry Wadsworth Longfellow.
John Quincy Adams.	James Russell Lowell.
William Cullen Bryant.	Ralph Waldo Emerson.
James Knox Polk.	James Abram Garfield.
Harrison Gray Otis.	John Jacob Astor.
William Ewart Gladstone.	George William Curtis.

LESSON VI.

COMPOSITION.

Write a statement answering each of the following questions: —

1. What is your name?
2. How old are you?
3. Have you brothers and sisters? If so, tell how many, and write their names.
4. Where is your home?
5. What school do you attend?
6. What is your teacher's name?
7. What can you do to make school pleasant?
8. When will your next vacation come?

Read your sentences carefully and correct any mistakes you may find. How many sentences have you written? Where have you used capitals? Where have you used periods? You may read what you have written.

To the Teacher. — All composition should be written under the immediate attention of the teacher. Guard against errors. Have some of the compositions read aloud to the class.

LESSON VII.

MEMORY EXERCISE.

Read the following poem with your teacher, and then commit it to memory: —

To the Teacher. — All poems should be read with the teacher *before* being committed to memory. In reading or reciting this poem, a boy may take the part of Robert and a girl that of Robin.

ROBIN AND ROBERT.

Robert.

O Robin, Robin bird,
    Wise as wise can be,
Why do you sit on that swinging bough,
    Nodding your head at me?
Haven't you any work to do,
    Hopping about all day?
Is it the whole of a Robin's life,
    To whistle and eat and play?

Robin.

O Robert, Robert boy,
    Why shouldn't I look at you?
If I am only a little bird,
    I have plenty of work to do.
Don't you whistle and eat and play,
    And play and whistle and eat?
Don't I see you at dinner-time,
    And out in the sunny street?

Robert.

Yes, but Robin, Robin bird,
    I study as well as play;
I'm half-way through my Reader now,
    And many a lesson I say.
But you don't have any books to read,
    And life you can enjoy.
I wish I were only a Robin bird,
    Instead of a Robert boy!

Robin.

Ah, Robert, Robert boy,
    You don't know what you say;
There's nobody longing to eat you up,
    Whenever you go to play;

There's nobody ready to hunt your nest,
  And steal you, if he could,
Or shoot you at sight with a horrid gun,
  When you wander in the wood.

But yonder the cat sits blinking
  Her great green eyes, you see;
She would break all the bones in my body,
  If she got her claws on me.
I never can be any other
  Than only a Robin, you know,
While you, perhaps, from a little boy,
  A tall, strong man will grow.

And you may win fame and honor,
  Wherever your name is heard,
But I shall never — no, never ! —
  Be anything but a bird.
So don't be idly wishing,
  For God knew best, you see,
When he made you a pretty Robert boy,
  Instead of a Robin like me.

LESSON VIII.

STORY FROM PICTURE.

Try to tell a story from the picture on page 13. If you need help, you may answer the following questions before you tell the story.

(Oral.)

1. To whom does the horse belong? What was the man doing when the horse started to run?

2. Where was the boy at work? What did he do when he saw the horse running? Was he hurt?

3. What did the man say to the boy? Did he offer to reward him? What reply did the boy make?

LESSON IX.

STORY FROM PICTURE.

(Written.)

You may now write a story about a runaway horse.

1. Tell who the man was, how he happened to leave his horse standing in the road, and what frightened the horse so that he ran away.

2. Tell about the little boy's working alone in the field, his jumping over the fence and catching hold of the horse's bridle.

3. Tell about the talk which the man had with the boy, and tell also what the boy said of his happy life though he was poor and obliged to work hard.

4. Finally, tell of the man's offering to pay the boy and the result.

LESSON X.

REPRODUCTION.

Read the following story carefully: —

THE MONKEY, THE CAT, AND THE CHESTNUTS.

A cat and a monkey sat one day by the fire. Their master had laid down some chestnuts before the blaze, and they had begun to crack with the heat. "Ah!" said the monkey, "how good those chestnuts smell! My dear friend, cat, your paws are made just like our master's hands. Why do you not try to pull a nut from the fire?"

The cat was so well pleased with what the monkey said, that she quite forgot to be careful. She put out her paw, and rolled a hot nut from the ashes. In doing this, she was burned a little, but what of that?

"How fine it is to have hands like a man!" said the cunning monkey. "Do try to get another nut!"

So the foolish cat put her paw into the hot ashes again and again, but when she turned for her share of the chestnuts, she found that the monkey had eaten them all.

Close your books and think about the story.

Write the story in your own words upon your slates or paper, first writing the title as it is in the book. You may begin your story with the words "Once upon a time."

Tell how the monkey managed to get the chestnuts. How did the cat feel when she thought it over afterwards? What do you think the story means?

LESSON XI.

IS AND ARE, WAS AND WERE.

Dictation Exercise.

1. The rat *is* in the pantry.
2. Two rats *are* in the pantry.
3. Harry *is* afraid of the rats.
4. Rob *is* afraid of the rats.
5. Harry and Rob *are* afraid of the rats.

Write the five foregoing statements as questions.

How many rats are spoken of in the first sentence, where we use *is?* in the second, where we use *are?* How many boys are spoken of in the third sentence? in the fourth? in the fifth?

Change the sentences, using *was* in place of *is*, and *were* in place of *are*.

Change the statements which you have just written into questions, using *was* and *were*.

Use *is* and *was* when speaking of one.
Use *are* and *were* when speaking of more than one.
Do not use *was* with *you*, either in statements or questions.

You were and *were you* are correct.

LESSON XII.

IS AND *ARE,* *WAS* AND *WERE* (*continued*).

Exercise.

(Oral and then Written.)

Read the rules at the end of Lesson XI. before beginning the following exercises.

Fill each blank with *is, are, was,* or *were:* —

1. —— the men at work now?
2. —— they at work yesterday?
3. I was at work, and so —— you.
4. Mary is here, but her sisters —— not.
5. —— James at school yesterday? —— you? No, but Fanny and Dot ——.
6. Six boys —— now playing ball. —— they playing this morning?
7. I am invited to the party. —— you? —— she? —— Ned and Henry?
8. I was invited to the party. —— you? —— she? —— Ned and Henry?
9. Maurice is to lose his recess. —— Rob? —— you? We —— not.
10. Maurice was to lose his recess. —— Rob? —— you? We —— not.
11. Where are the boys to-day? Where —— they yesterday?
12. Where —— you girls last Monday? We —— at school.

LESSON XIII.

STORY FROM PICTURE.

(Oral.)

Tell what you can see in the larger picture on page 17; in the smaller.

Begin a story with, "One pleasant morning." Tell

about the bird, where he found the tub, and why he went to it. What happened afterward? What did the cat think, and what did she do? Was she disappointed? Does the cat look pleased in the second picture?

There is a very old saying, "Look before you leap." What do you think of it?

LESSON XIV.

STORY FROM PICTURE.

(Written.)

Write the story about the bird and the cat. Give them each a name. Write, for the title of your story, *Look Before You Leap*.

To THE TEACHER. — For class criticism, two or three of these stories may be written on the board while others are being written on slates or paper.

LESSON XV.

ABOUT GAMES.

(Oral.)

Think about the games you know. Give the names of three or four of them. Which one do you like best? Tell just how one of them is played, so that any one not knowing the game may learn it from you.

LESSON XVI.

MEMORY EXERCISE.

Commit to memory and recite the following poem: —

WHAT ROBIN TOLD.

How do the robins build their nest?
  Robin Redbreast told me.
First a wisp of yellow hay
In a pretty round they lay;
Then some shreds of downy floss,
Feathers too, and bits of moss,
Woven with a sweet, sweet song,
This way, that way, and across:
That's what Robin told me.

Where do the robins hide their nest?
  Robin Redbreast told me.
Up among the leaves so deep,
Where the sunbeams rarely creep.
Long before the winds are cold,
Long before the leaves are gold,
Bright-eyed stars will peep and see
Baby robins — one, two, three:
That's what Robin told me.

In this poem, you will notice two divisions of nine lines each. These divisions are called **stanzas.**

The number of lines in a stanza varies in different poems.

What does the first stanza tell about? the first part of the second? the last part of the second?

LESSON XVII.

DAYS OF THE WEEK.

Carefully study the spelling of the names of the days. Then learn the abbreviations for the names: —

NAMES.	ABBREVIATIONS.
Sunday.	Sun.
Monday.	Mon.
Tuesday.	Tues.
Wednesday.	Wed.
Thursday.	Thurs.
Friday.	Fri.
Saturday.	Sat.

The names of the days should always begin with capitals. Always place a period after an abbreviation.

Dictation Exercise.

1. On Saturday and Sunday there is no school.
2. Last Monday it rained, but we were at school.
3. Where were you Tuesday and Wednesday? We were at school.
4. Thursday and Friday were holidays.

To THE TEACHER. — For a second dictation lesson, give the same sentences, but require abbreviations of the names of the days.

LESSON XVIII.

MONTHS OF THE YEAR.

Learn these names and abbreviations: —

January,	Jan.	July,	———
February,	Feb.	August,	Aug.
March,	Mar	September,	Sept.
April,	Apr.	October,	Oct.
May,	———	November,	Nov.
June,	———	December,	Dec.

How to Write Dates.

"July 4, 1776" is called a date. In writing dates, place a comma after the day of the month. Notice that the names of three of the months are not abbreviated.

Dictation Exercise.

1. Washington was born Feb. 22, 1732.
2. What happened July 4, 1776?
3. Columbus landed in America Oct. 14, 1492.
4. Washington was in New York April 30, 1789.
5. The Pilgrims landed Dec. 21, 1620.

Write in a sentence the date of your last birthday.

LESSON XIX.

STORY FROM PICTURE.

If I had to write a story about the pictures on page 21, I should think who the children were. I should tell about their old dog; what fun they had with him; how dogs and cats dislike each other; and what happened.

I think *A Lively Ride* would be a good name for the story. Write the story and make it the best one you have ever written.

LESSON XX.

THERE ARE AND THERE WERE.

Remember that *is* and *was* should be used when speaking of one, and *are* and *were* when speaking of more than one.

Exercise.
(Oral and then Written.)

Think carefully before filling the following blanks with *is*, *are*, *was*, or *were*.

1. There —— one tree in our yard.
2. There —— three trees in the school yard.
3. Yesterday there —— only one session of school.

4. I thought there —— two.
5. —— there a horse in the road? No, but there —— several an hour ago.
6. —— there many rainy days last month? No, there —— only two.
7. Where —— the birds last January? They —— in the South.
8. Where —— they now? They —— all about us.

LESSON XXI.

REPRODUCTION.

A Bird's Story.

I built me a nest in the old oak tree —
As pretty a nest as ever could be.
I wove it with threads to the oak-tree bough;
And three little birdies are sleeping there now.

One day as I sang my "Cheer up, chee, chee,"
A spry little squirrel sprang up in the tree.
I thought he was coming right up on the bough —
It makes my heart tremble to think of it now.

I flew like an eagle right down through the air;
And soon he was running, he did not know where.
I pecked him and pecked him, and flew in his track;
I am sure he will be in no haste to come back.

Tell in your own words about the bird's building her nest. What sort of bird do you think it was? What color were her eggs? How many little birdies were there? The little birds' mouths are open; are they singing?

"One day" what happened? Do you think the squirrel meant to harm the little birds?

LESSON XXII.

COMPOSITION.

Write in your own words the story of *The Mother Bird and the Squirrel.*

LESSON XXIII.

MEMORY EXERCISE.

Read the following poem and commit it to memory:—

A Song.

Scatter in springtime a handful of seeds,
    And gather in summer a lapful of flowers.
    This is the song of the birds in the bowers,
This is the song of the wind in the reeds.

Down by the roadside and over the meads,
    Under the sunshine and under the showers,
Scatter in springtime a handful of seeds,
    And gather in summer a lapful of flowers.

Scatter in childhood kind words and kind deeds,
    Scatter them everywhere through all the hours;
    Whether sky brightens or whether cloud lowers,
Their blossoms shall come to thee ere summer speeds.
Scatter in springtime a handful of seeds,
    And gather in summer a lapful of flowers.

CHAPTER II.

LESSON XXIV.

ORAL LESSON FROM PICTURE.

(*Seeing.*) What can you see in this picture?
(*Thinking.*) What is the time of year? Is the story about the country or the city?
Who is near the horses? Who are on the load of hay?

(*Thinking.*) Where are visitors from? How did they get to the farm?
Where is this load of hay going? Of what use is it?
Is it all fun in the hayfield?
(*Telling.*) Tell the story suggested by the picture.

LESSON XXV.

TO, TOO, AND TWO.

These are three of the hardest words in our language for children to learn. Many never learn to write them correctly.

To indicates *motion towards*. *Two* is a *number*. *Too* means *also*, or *more than enough*.

If you think before you write, you will not be likely to make a mistake in using these words. The following sentences are correct: —

Examples: I went *to* town yesterday.
I stayed there only *two* hours.
I could not stay longer, because I was *too* tired.

Exercise.

(Oral and then Written.)

Fill each of the following blanks with the right word: —

1. —— weeks make a fortnight.
2. There is —— much noise in the room.
3. The book cost —— dollars.
4. Mother said it cost —— much.
5. I thought so, ——.
6. —— boys fell from the tree —— the ground.
7. They were —— eager —— get down.

LESSON XXVI.

THERE AND THEIR.

Here are two more words very hard to use correctly. *Their* always denotes *ownership*. *There* often denotes *place*, never ownership.

Examples: There are the boys.
Is *their* father with them?

Exercise.

Use the right words in these blanks: —

1. —— are nine of our boys playing ball.
2. —— teacher is keeping the score.
3. The boys are improving —— holiday.
4. Look ——! Tom made a home run.
5. The squirrel is up —— in the tree.
6. Ned and Rob are visiting —— cousin.

LESSON XXVII.

REPRODUCTION.

A man named Æsop wrote fables more than two thousand years ago. Here is one of them, which you may read carefully, and then write in your own words.

The Lion and the Fox.

A Lion that had grown old, and had no more strength to forage for food, saw that he must get it by cunning. He went into his den and crept into a corner, and made believe that he was very sick.

All the animals about came in to take a look at him, and, as they came, he snapped them up. Now, when a good many beasts had been caught in this way, the Fox, who guessed the trick, came along. He

VOWEL EXERCISE. 27

took his stand a little way from the den, and asked the Lion how he was.

The Lion said he was very sick, and begged the Fox to come into the den and see him.

"So I would," said the Fox, "but I notice that all the footprints point into the den, and there are none that point out."

LESSON XXVIII.

VOWEL EXERCISE.

(Oral.)

Our alphabet has twenty-six letters.

Five of these letters, *a, e, i, o,* and *u,* are called **vowels**.

Notice the different sounds of *a* in l*a*me and l*a*mb; of *e* in m*e* and m*e*t; of *i* in w*i*ne and w*i*n; of *o* in wr*o*te and r*o*t; of *u* in f*u*me and f*u*n.

Speak each pair of words above, and then the vowel sounds in them.

1. From the following list, select the words having the same sound of *a:*

cap, cape, lane, male, fat, man, grate, take, at, have.

How many different sounds has *a* in the ten words?

2. Select the words having the same sound of *e:*

red, pet, feet, tree, mean, stem, head, steam, see, set.

How many different sounds has *e* in these words?

3. Select the words having the same sound of *i:*

fine, thine, limb, climb, pine, mine, rip, ripe, win, wine.

How many different sounds of *i* do you find?

4. Select the words having the same sound of *o*:

    note, not, lot, coat, comb, stop, throw, go, got, drove.

How many different sounds of *o* do you find?

5. Select words having the same sound of *u*:

    tune, flute, tub, cut, tube, cube, blunt, hum, thumb, June.

How many different sounds has *u* in these words?

LESSON XXIX.

VOWEL EXERCISE (*continued*).

In the dictionary, a mark placed above or below a vowel shows what sound should be given to it. This aids us in pronouncing the word correctly.

The two most common marks are the **macron** (-) to show the long sound, and the **breve** (˘) to show the short sound.

The vowels in the following words are correctly marked:

    āte, ăt; stēam, stĕm; hīde, hĭd; hōle, hŏt; tūne, tŭb.

Give the long and the short sound of each vowel by itself.

Now write the words in the five lists in Lesson XXVIII. and place a macron or a breve over the proper letter in each.

Tell whether the vowels in the following words are long or short.

Copy the words upon your slate and place over each vowel the proper mark.

in	hush	us	red	old
sing	from	day	way	upon
chubby	bring	tell	socks	rustling
think	waking	when	have	behind

LESSON XXX.

MEMORY EXERCISE.

Read the following poem with your teacher. Then commit it to memory and recite it: —

MERRY CHRISTMAS.

In the hush of early morning,
    When the red burns through the gray,
And the wintry world lies waiting
    For the glory of the day,
Then we hear a fitful rustling
    Just without upon the stair,
See two small white phantoms coming,
    Catch the gleam of sunny hair.

Are they Christmas fairies stealing
    Rows of little socks to fill?
Are they angels floating hither
    With their message of good will?
What sweet spells are these elves weaving,
    As like larks they chirp and sing?
Are these palms of peace from heaven
    That these lovely spirits bring?

Rosy feet upon the threshold,
    Eager faces peeping through,
With the first red ray of sunshine,
    Chanting cherubs come in view:
Mistletoe and gleaming holly,
    Symbols of a blessed day,
In their chubby hands they carry,
    Streaming all along the way.

Well we know them, never weary
    Of this innocent surprise, —
Waiting, watching, listening always
    With full hearts and tender eyes,

> While our little household angels,
> White and golden in the sun,
> Greet us with the sweet old welcome, —
> "Merry Christmas, every one!"
>
> —Louisa M. Alcott.

LESSON XXXI.

SYLLABLES.

The word *come* has one syllable.
The word *be-come* has two syllables.
The word *be-com-ing* has three syllables.
The word *un-be-com-ing* has four syllables.
The word *un-be-com-ing-ly* has five syllables.

Speak the following words slowly and distinctly, and tell how many syllables each has: —

using	many	family	butterfly
write	following	letter	comfort
syllable	distinctly	vowel	written
reader	language	speak	comforting

Copy the words, placing those of one syllable in one column, those of two syllables in another, and those of three syllables in another. Separate the syllables as you copy; thus, *sep-a-rate*.

A word of one syllable is spoken with one impulse of the voice; as, *come*. A word of two syllables is spoken with two impulses of the voice; as, *be-come*. A word of three syllables, with three impulses; as, *be-com-ing*.

When part of a word is written on one line, and the rest on the next, the division must be made between syllables, and the former line must be closed with a hyphen.

DICTATION.

LESSON XXXII.

SYLLABLES (*continued*).

Answer in sentences: —
How many syllables are there in the name of each day of the week? How many syllables are there in the name of each month? How many syllables are there in each word of your name?

Sometimes *y* has the sound of *i*; as, *sly, fly, my, lyre, tyrant*.

In *slyly*, the first *y* sounds like long *i*, and the second like short *i*.

When *y* has the sound of *i*, it is a vowel.

Can you find on this page a word which has no vowel in it?

See whether in the names of the days of the week and the months of the year, each syllable has at least one vowel in it.

> A word of one syllable is a monosyllable.
> A word of two syllables is a dissyllable.
> A word of three syllables is a trisyllable.
> A word of more than three syllables is a polysyllable.

LESSON XXXIII.

DICTATION.

Study carefully the spelling, capitals, and punctuation in this lesson: —

Deaf and dumb people can neither speak nor hear. They have a sign language. Did you ever see them use this language? Do they talk rapidly with it? Can you talk with your fingers?

Many deaf mutes have been taught to speak. Then they are no longer mutes. Have you ever heard them talk?

Answer the following questions in complete sentences: —

Which words in the dictation exercise are dissyllables? Which are trisyllables? How many are monosyllables? Is there a polysyllable?

In *rapidly*, why is *y* a vowel? In this lesson what other words can you find that contain the letter *y* used as a vowel? Tell in each case whether it represents long *i* or short *i*. Give a reason for each punctuation mark. Why are the capitals used? What are mutes? What are deaf mutes?

LESSON XXXIV.

STORY FROM PICTURE.

(Oral and then Written.)

This picture shows that a mouse once had a rather lively time. Suppose he were to tell the story himself, what do you think he might say? You may write the story.

ANIMALS AND PLANTS.

LESSON XXXV.

ANIMALS.

Answer the following questions in oral sentences: —

1. Are birds, fishes, and insects animals?
2. Which do you think are the five most useful animals?
3. Tell why each is useful.
4. What is the largest animal that you have seen?
5. Of what use, if any, is he to man?
6. Tell something that you have heard or read about this animal.
7. What sort of food does the elephant eat?
8. How does he get it into his mouth?
9. Tell why some animals have claws.
10. What are "beasts of prey"?

LESSON XXXVI.

PLANTS.

In answering the following questions, make complete statements: —

1. Name five important food plants.
2. Which plant do you think feeds the most people?
3. Name three plants that are useful for clothing.
4. What is the largest plant that you have seen?
5. Give some of its uses.
6. Name some large plants that grow from small seeds.
7. Name some plants that are cultivated only because they are beautiful.
8. Do you think such plants are useful? Why?

LESSON XXXVII.

MEMORY EXERCISE.

Commit to memory and recite the following poem: —

Waiting to Grow.

Little white snowdrops, just waking up,
Violet, daisy, and sweet buttercup!
Think of the flowers that are under the snow,
  Waiting to grow!

And think what hosts of queer little seeds,
Of flowers and mosses, of ferns and of weeds,
Are under the leaves and under the snow,
  Waiting to grow!

Think of the roots getting ready to sprout,
Reaching their slender, brown fingers about
Under the ice and the leaves and the snow,
  Waiting to grow!

Only a month, or a few weeks more,
Will they have to wait behind that door,
Listen and watch and wait below,
  Waiting to grow!

Nothing so small, and hidden so well,
That God will not find it and presently tell
His sun where to shine and his rain where to go,
  Helping them grow!

1. How many of the flowers mentioned in this poem have you seen?
2. Tell the color of each one.
3. What makes them grow, and why will they not grow in the winter?
4. Write the poem from memory.

LESSON XXXVIII.

INFORMATION LESSON.

CHERRY BUDS.

With a sprig containing a cherry bud partly open in your hand, read the following description, and see if you can find all the parts that are mentioned.

Make a note of everything you can see which is not mentioned in the description.

If you look at the sprigs of a cherry tree in April or May, you will find on them many round buds of a brownish color. Soon the brown scales of the buds are pushed apart, and out come the beautiful white flowers and the green leaves, which have all been packed inside the buds.

Away down in the center of the flower is a little shining green bud, which is a baby cherry. When all the other parts of the flower have withered and dropped off, this little cherry grows very fast, until it is ripe and ready to be eaten.

After the tree has ripened its cherries, it has other work to do through the summer. It must get ready some new buds to make blossoms and cherries for another year. These buds are quite small and may be found just where the stems of the leaves join the twigs. They are wrapped so carefully in brown scales that the cold winter does them no harm; and, though they show no signs of life for several months, they are ready to wake in the warm spring sun and unpack their flowers and leaves. — H. L. CLAPP.

Place the sprigs of cherry in water for a day or two.

LESSON XXXIX.

INFORMATION LESSON (*continued*).

TOPICS FOR CONVERSATION.

Why should this lesson be studied in the spring? What fruit trees have you seen in blossom earlier than the cherry? What are the size and shape of the cherry bud? What is the color of the blossom? Why could you not see the flowers and green leaves when you examined the bud? Where was the little cherry? Why does it grow so rapidly after the flower withers? When will it be ripe and ready for eating?

What work is done by the cherry tree after its fruit is ripened? Where may the cherry buds for the following year be found? How are they preserved during the cold winter?

Notice carefully all the parts of the cherry bud, and describe them in the best sentences you can make.

TO THE TEACHER. — While describing the cherry buds, each pupil should have a sprig of cherry in his hand.

LESSON XL.

COMPOSITION.

Write what you have learned about cherry buds, making such use as you please of the topics in the preceding lesson.

Tell some of the uses made of the fruit of the cherry tree.

LESSON XLI.

MEMORY EXERCISE.

Read the following poem with your teacher and then commit it to memory: —

THE TREE.

The Tree's early leaf-buds were bursting their brown;
"Shall I take them away?" said the Frost, sweeping down.
"No, leave them alone
Till the blossoms have grown,"
Prayed the Tree, while he trembled from rootlet to crown.

The Tree bore his blossoms, and all the birds sung.
"Shall I take them away?" said the Wind as he swung.
"No, leave them alone
Till the berries have grown,"
Said the Tree, while his leaflets quivering hung.

The Tree bore his fruit in the midsummer glow.
Said the girl, "May I gather thy ripe berries now?"
"Yes, all thou canst see.
Take them; all are for thee,"
Said the Tree, while he bent down his laden boughs low.

— BJÖRNSTJERNE BJÖRNSON.

Read carefully, and answer the following questions in sentences: —

1. What were the "leaf-buds"? What is meant by "bursting their brown"? What did the Frost say? What did he mean? What did the Tree answer? Did the Frost take the leaf-buds away? How do you know?

2. Why did all the birds sing? What did the Wind ask? What did he mean? What did the Tree answer? Did the Wind do as the Tree wished? How do you know?

3. What is "midsummer"? When is it? What is meant by "glow"? What did the girl ask? What did the Tree answer? What is meant by "laden boughs"? What kind of tree may it have been? Give a reason for your answer.

LESSON XLII.

OUR FLAG.

(Oral.)

Tell what you can of each topic mentioned below.

The shape of the flag. The colors in it. Its different parts. What is the *field?* Its color. The number and color of the stripes. The number and color of the stars.

Does the number of stripes ever change? Why? Does the num-

STORY FROM PICTURE. 39

ber of stars ever change? Why? How many stars were on the flag at first? Find out other facts connected with the history of our flag. Do you think there will be still more stars?

Has the flag any use? Where is it used? What names are given to it? Has your schoolhouse a flag? If so, on what days should it be raised? How can you honor " Our Flag"?

To THE TEACHER. — A flag should hang before the class during the lesson.

LESSON XLIII.

STORY FROM PICTURE.

Write a story from the picture above, using the following hints: —

The little boy and girl that you see in the picture are brother and sister. Where do they live? Do you think they are playing truant, or is it a holiday? Which is older, the boy or the girl, and what are their names?

They have been out playing and have found a strange dog. I wonder what has happened to him! They found him lying by the side of the road and crying piteously. He looked up at them as though he would like to tell them what had happened. The children could hear the noise of a carriage that had just been driven by. Has the dog been run over, or has he been bitten by another dog? What are the children trying to do? Why do they pity the poor dog?

When they have bound up the poor dog's foot, do you suppose they will take him to their own home? What a nice playfellow he will make if he gets well!

LESSON XLIV.

PRONUNCIATION AND CLASSIFICATION.

Pronounce very distinctly the following words according to the marking: —

whōle	slēēk	bīte	bŭtter
nōbŏdў	bădе	pĕtal	hŏrrĭd
drāin	pātrĭot	fōrge	sĭttĭng
mĭnnōws	vĭctorў	tūbe	hăppĭnĕss

Write in separate columns the monosyllables, the dissyllables, and the trisyllables.

Use each word in an oral sentence, speaking very distinctly.

Mark the vowels in the following words: —

red	met	ripen	music
pin	rain	carry	brave
both	bank	borrow	kingly
meet	time	evening	children

LESSON XLV.

MEMORY EXERCISE.

Commit to memory and recite the following poem: —

GRANDPAPA.

Grandpapa's hair is very white,
    And grandpapa walks but slow;
He likes to sit still in his easy-chair,
    While the children come and go.
"Hush! play quietly," says mamma;
"Let nobody trouble dear grandpapa."

Grandpapa's hand is thin and weak;
    It has worked hard all his days,—
A strong right hand and an honest hand,
    That has won all good men's praise.
"Kiss it tenderly," says mamma;
"Let every one honor grandpapa."

Grandpapa's eyes are growing dim;
    They have looked on sorrow and death;
But the love-light never went out of them,
    Nor the courage and the faith.
"You, children, all of you," says mamma,
"Have need to look up to dear grandpapa."

Grandpapa's years are wearing few,
    But he leaves a blessing behind.
A good life lived, and a good fight fought,
    True heart and equal mind.
"Remember, my children," says mamma,
"You bear the name of your grandpapa."

                              — MRS. CRAIK.

Tell in your own words all you can about the grandpapa of the poem. Tell something about any grandpapa that you know or have known.

LESSON XLVI.

COMPOSITION WRITING.

While learning to write compositions, here are six good rules to have always in mind: —

1. Be sure that each thought is complete before beginning to write it in a sentence.
2. Be sure to begin each sentence with a capital.
3. Be sure to punctuate every sentence.
4. Write as well as you can.
5. If you have any doubt whatever about the spelling of a word, find it in the dictionary, or ask to have it written on the blackboard.
6. Do not try to write too much.

COMPOSITION.

Write about a snowstorm that you remember, using any of these notes you choose: —

When it was; where you were; what you were doing; whether the wind blew and whistled; whether much snow fell, and great drifts formed; what made them; what sport the snow furnished you, and what work.

Does the snow do any good? If so, what?

In writing the foregoing story about a snowstorm, have you kept in mind the six rules given above? What rule do you think you have broken?

To the Teacher. — Read to the pupils the whole or a part of Whittier's "Snow Bound." Let them describe the work and the play which the poet tells about, and then describe their own work or play as required in the notes.

LESSON XLVII.

STORY FROM PICTURE.

(Oral and then Written.)

Tell what you can see in the pictures, and what you think it all means.

Write the story, giving names to the children and to the doll.

Remember the rules in Lesson XLVI.

Tell where these children live, and to whom the "doctor's" clothes belong. What has he in his hand, and what is he trying to do with it?

What will be a good name for this story?

LESSON XLVIII.

COVERINGS OF ANIMALS.

(Oral.)

The covering of an animal is a part of the animal, just as the bark is a part of the tree. Let us think about the different coverings of different animals, of their uses to the animals, and of their uses to man.

1. What covering has an oyster? Describe it. What is its use?
2. What covering has a dog? a cat? How do they differ? What are the uses of these coverings?
3. What covering has a snail? What is its use?
4. What covering has a fish? Describe the parts; tell how they are put on, and why they are so put on.
5. What covering has a sheep? What uses are made of this covering?
6. What articles of clothing are made from the coverings of animals?

LESSON XLIX.

REPRODUCTION.

Here is another fable from Æsop. Read it carefully and then write it in your own words.

The Four Bulls and the Lion.

Four bulls once agreed to live together, and they fed in the same pasture. Now the lion saw them afar off, and wanted to hunt them, but he knew that he could not, so long as they held together.

So he managed to set them quarreling with each other; and when that happened, they separated, and he easily mastered them, one at a time.

CHAPTER III.

LESSON L.

PROPER NAMES.

The special name given to any person, place, or thing is called a **proper name**; as, *John Adams*, *Chicago*, *North America*.

Every word in a proper name must begin with a capital letter.[1]

Dictation Exercise.

Study the following sentences so that you can write each correctly from one reading. Draw a line under the proper name or names in each sentence that you have written.

1. James A. Garfield was a poor boy.
2. He lived in Ohio.
3. Young Garfield drove horses on a tow path.
4. He became President of the United States.
5. Abraham Lincoln was born in Kentucky.
6. He moved to Illinois.
7. Lincoln lived in a log cabin when a boy.
8. He is sometimes called the "Martyr President."
9. Bunker Hill monument is on Breed's Hill.
10. The battle was fought on Breed's Hill.
11. St. Louis is on the Mississippi River.
12. The city of New Orleans is near the Gulf of Mexico.

[1] In names like *The United States of America* and *Simon de Montford*, however, the words *of* and *de* do not begin with capitals.

LESSON LI.

PROPER NAMES (*continued*).

Write five sentences, each containing the name of a boy whom you know, and the name of the place where he lives.

Write the names of five girls whom you know.

Write five questions, using the names of persons in this room.

What proper nouns have you used in each sentence?

What mark have you used after each sentence? Why?

Give two rules for the capitals you have used.

LESSON LII.

NAMES AND DATES.

(Oral and then Written.)

Be sure of the capitals and of the spelling of the words that you use in writing the answers to the following questions: —

Answer in complete sentences, and use no abbreviations

1. When is your birthday?
2. On what date is Christmas?
3. Which is the shortest month?
4. Which months have thirty-one days?
5. Which months have thirty days?
6. Which is the middle day of the week?
7. On which days is there no school?
8. On which day of the week are your lessons poorest?
9. When is Washington's birthday?
10. On what date are you answering this question?

LESSON LIII.

STORY FROM PICTURE.

(Oral and then Written.)

Tell a story from this picture. The girl, the boy, and the dog are the same that you saw on page 39.

SUGGESTIONS.

What have the children been doing? Did the sticks float down the stream? What did Carlo do? What was the little girl trying to do when she fell off the bridge? Why did Carlo plunge into the water. after the little girl? What might have happened?

Was the little girl sick for a long time? I wonder whether Carlo used to go into the sick-room to see her! Do you suppose that papa and mamma were sorry that the children had taken pity on the poor, lame dog?

LESSON LIV.

VOWEL SOUNDS.

Some of the vowels have other sounds besides the long and the short sounds.

The letter *a* has a different sound in each of these words: —

cāne   căn   tạll   fär   àsk

You know the names of the first two sounds of *a*. The third is called *broad a*, and the fourth *Italian a*. The fifth sound is the hardest of all to learn. It is just midway between *short a* and *Italian a*. It occurs in such words as

àsk   gràss   brànch   dànce   glàss   tàsk

Tell which of the following words have *broad a* and which have *Italian a*: —

far	fall	are	palm	talk
all	star	squall	mark	hard

Mark the *a* in each word.

Write five other words containing *broad a*, and five containing *Italian a*.

LESSON LV.

VOWEL SOUNDS (*continued*).

The sounds of *o* in **mọve**, *oo* in **mōōn**, and *u* in **rụde**, are all exactly alike. The sound is called *long oo*, and the vowels are marked as you see them.

The sounds of *o* in **wọlf**, *oo* in **fŏŏt**, and *u* in **bụll**, are all alike. The sound is called *short oo*.

MEMORY EXERCISE.

Pronounce the following words with the *long oo* sound, and tell how the vowels should be marked: —

whose   soon   true   prove   do
room   fruit canoe   rule   brute

Pronounce the following words with the *short oo* sound, and tell how the vowels should be marked: —

push   good   foot   pull   woman

LESSON LVI.

MEMORY EXERCISE.

Commit to memory and recite the following poem:—

DANDELION.

There's a dandy little fellow
Who dresses all in yellow, —
In yellow, with an overcoat of green;
With his hair all crisp and curly,
In the springtime bright and early,—
Tripping o'er the meadow he is seen.
Through all the bright June weather,
Like a jolly little tramp
He wanders o'er the hillside, down the road;
Around his yellow feather
The gypsy fireflies camp;
His companions are the wood lark and the toad.
Spick and spandy, little dandy,
Golden dancer in the dell!
Green and yellow, happy fellow,
All the little children love him well!

But at last this little fellow
Doffs his dandy coat of yellow,
And very feebly totters o'er the green; —
For he very old is growing,

INFORMATION LESSON.

And, with hair all white and flowing,
A-nodding in the sunlight he is seen.
  The little winds of morning
  Come a-flying through the grass,
And clap their hands around him in their glee;
  They shake him without warning;
  His wig falls off, alas!
And a little baldhead dandy now is he.
  Oh, poor dandy, once so spandy,
  Golden dancer on the lea!
  Older growing, white hair flowing,
  Poor little baldhead dandy now is he!

To the Teacher. — Conversation suggested by this little poem should make an excellent language lesson.

LESSON LVII.

INFORMATION LESSON.

(Oral and then Written.)

Read carefully this account of the fly. Notice flies as you see them about the house, and read anything else about them that you can find.

A Talk about Flies.

The body of a fly has three parts, one of which is the head. On its head are two large eyes. But what will you think when I tell you that each of these large eyes is made up of about four thousand small eyes?

Each of the small eyes has six sides. Of course these tiny eyes are placed very close to each other, for the four thousand together are not so large as a pin-head. Is it any wonder that the fly is so hard to catch? It can see every way at the same time.

Eyes of a Fly.

Small Eyes of a Fly.

INFORMATION LESSON.

The fly's feet are also very curious. They are made so that it can walk on the wall of a room as well as on the floor; and it can even run up and down the glass in our windows.

The fly has no teeth. Its mouth is a kind of trunk, through which it sucks its food. It cannot eat anything that is hard. Still, you know that flies are very fond of sugar, and you want to know how they can eat that. They have something to drop upon the sugar, which softens it into a sirup; then they draw this sirup up through their trunks.

Flies do not breathe through their noses: I do not know that they have noses. They breathe through little holes in their sides.

I have only one thing more to tell you about this curious little creature. It always keeps itself very clean. Have you ever seen a fly rub its front legs over its head? I suppose you have often wondered why it does this.

The under side of the fly's feet and its legs have tiny hairs on them. These are its hair-brushes, which it always carries ready for use. If any dirt gets on its head or face, it brushes it off. Then it rubs its feet and legs together so that no dirt shall stick to them.

LEG OF A FLY.

Do you not think that there are many boys and girls who may learn something even from a fly? What may the fly teach us?

HARPER'S SECOND READER.

TOPICS FOR CONVERSATION.

The fly is an insect. Why? Its body. Its eyes. Its feet. Has it any teeth? Its mouth, and how it eats. How it eats sugar. How it breathes. Its cleanliness. What have you noticed about the fly? What else have you read about it?

What other kinds of flies, besides house-flies, have you seen? Tell how the fly differs from the mosquito. Which gives us the most trouble, and why?

LESSON LVIII.

SILENT LETTERS.

In the word *high*, only the first two letters are sounded when the word is spoken. The last two are silent letters. In *band* all of the letters are sounded. In *mine* the *e* is silent. In *through* there are seven letters and only three sounds. In *leave* there are five letters and only three sounds.

Exercise.

Tell which of the following words have all of the letters sounded and which words have silent letters: —

barn	tail	are	write
lane	trim	two	last
lean	glum	have	lamp
pink	thumb	night	could

How many letters are there in each word? How many sounds?

Name other words that have silent letters, and tell which letters are silent.

LESSON LIX.

ACCENTED SYLLABLES.

Words of more than one syllable have what is called an accented syllable; that is, a syllable which is pronounced with a stronger impulse of the voice than the others in the same word. Thus in the words *yesterday, playing, garden*, the first syllables are accented. In the dictionaries such syllables are marked as follows: —

   yĕs' ter day plāy' ing gär' den

PRONUNCIATION. 53

Separate the following words into syllables, and mark the accented syllable in each: —

delay	belong	differ	syllable
honest	believe	must	incomplete
letters	follow	butterfly	behave

Write the words of two syllables in a column; the words of three syllables.

Mark the vowel in each accented syllable.

Why is *y* a vowel in the word *syllable?*

Select words of two syllables from your reading lesson, and tell which syllable is accented in each.

LESSON LX.

PRONUNCIATION.

Pronounce distinctly the following words as they are marked: —

clåss	sạu' cy	roof' less	wĭn' dōw
heärth	kĕt' tle	re cĕss'	stămp' ing
rōōt	chànce	chĭl' drĕn	ba nä' nå

Tell which words are monosyllables, which dissyllables, and which trisyllables.

Name the vowel sounds which are marked.

Name those marked in Lesson XLIV.

Use each word in an oral sentence.

Write the words when pronounced, and mark from memory the vowel in each monosyllable and in each accented syllable of the remaining words.

Mark some vowels in words taken from your oral sentences.

To the Teacher. — The word *a*, when emphatic, has the sound of *long a;* when not emphatic, of *ȧ*.

The should rarely be spoken with the full sound of *long e*. Indeed, when before a consonant, the vowel is nearly *short u*.

LESSON LXI.

REPRODUCTION.

Read the following story carefully; then close the book, think the story over, and write it as well as you can.

What name will you select for the story?

A Newfoundland dog and a mastiff had a quarrel. The dogs were fighting on a 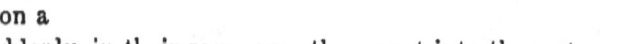 bridge, and suddenly, in their rage, over they went into the water.

The banks were so high that they were forced to swim a long distance before they came to a landing-place. This was easy for the Newfoundland dog. He was as much at home in the water as a seal. But not so with poor Bruce.

Old Bravo, the Newfoundland, had reached the bank, and turned to look at his enemy. He saw that the other dog, whose strength was fast failing, was likely to drown. So he plunged in, seized the mastiff gently by the collar, and towed the poor fellow safely into port.

LESSON LXII.

MEMORY EXERCISE.

Commit to memory and recite the following poem: —

>Have you heard the waters singing,
>   Little May,
>Where the willows green are leaning
>   O'er their way?
>Do you know how low and sweet,
>O'er the pebbles at their feet,
>Are the words the waves repeat,
>   Night and day?
>
>Have you heard the robins singing,
>   Little one,
>Where the rosy day is breaking —
>   When 'tis done?
>Have you heard the wooing breeze,
>In the blossomed orchard trees,
>And the drowsy hum of bees
>   In the sun?
>
>All the earth is full of music,
>   Little May;
>Bird and bee, and water singing
>   On its way.
>Let their silver voices fall
>On thy heart with happy call:
>"Praise the Lord, who loveth all,
>   Night and day."

1. Tell what is meant by "the waters singing."
2. In the fourth line, whose way is "their way"?
3. In the sixth line, whose "feet" are referred to?
4. Tell about the kinds of music with which the earth is filled.

LESSON LXIII.

SEEDS AND PLANTS.

(Oral and then Written.)

1. In which season of the year does the farmer plant seed?
2. Mention a few of the kinds of seed that he plants.
3. How must the ground be prepared before planting?
4. Of what use is the root of the plant?
5. Why does a very large tree have very large roots?
6. Mention a small plant that has a large root.
7. Name some roots that are good to eat.
8. Of what use are the leaves of a plant?
9. Are the leaves ever used for food?

COMPOSITION.

Write all that the foregoing questions suggest to you about seeds and plants.

LESSON LXIV.

PRONUNCIATION.

(Oral and Written.)

Pronounce the following words as they are marked:—

rule	vī' o let	cătch
sĭn' gu lar	hŭn' drĕd	ŏff
be cause'	glȧnce	pȧ pä'
bŏn' net	făc' to ry	mȧm mä'

Use each word in a complete oral sentence which shall show that you know the meaning of the word.

Tell how many syllables each word has, and why.

STORY FROM PICTURE. 57

Write the following words, separating the syllables, and marking the vowel of each accented syllable.

Boston	piano	inquiry
Baltimore	florist	interesting
Chicago	address	estimate

LESSON LXV.

STORY FROM PICTURE.

(Oral and then Written.)

Tell what you see in the picture: how the boys look; what time of year it is, and how you know; where you think the boys are going; what seems to be going on; and what you think of it.

Write a story, giving names to the boys. Tell about the poor boy and his home.

LESSON LXVI.

DICTATION EXERCISE.

Study spelling, capitals, and punctuation: —

Everything in the world is *animal*, *vegetable*, or *mineral*. Things that we get from animals are called animal productions. Things that we get from plants are vegetable productions. Everything else is mineral. So there are three classes of objects. When we say a thing is animal, vegetable, or mineral, we classify it.

Oral Exercise.

Classify the objects named below: —

moss	salt	cotton	leather	hair
coral	pepper	stone	bread	milk
pearl	eggs	coffee	ivory	water

LESSON LXVII.

WORDS AND THEIR OPPOSITES.

Name a word having a meaning opposite to each of the following and use it in a sentence: —

rough	right	good	tall	long
sweet	east	wide	fat	swift
brittle	north	deep	thick	clean

LESSON LXVIII.

STUDY OF POEM.

THE WIND AND THE LEAVES.

"Come, little leaves," said the wind one day,
"Come o'er the meadows with me, and play.
Put on your dresses of red and gold; —
Summer is gone, and the days grow cold."

STUDY OF POEM.

Soon as the leaves heard the wind's low call,
Down they came fluttering, one and all;
Over the brown fields they danced and flew,
Singing the soft little songs they knew.

"Cricket, good-by, we've been friends so long!
Pretty brook, sing us your farewell song; —
Say you are sorry to see us go.
Oh! you will miss us, right well we know.

"Dear little lambs, in your fleecy fold,
Mother will keep you from harm and cold;
Fondly we've watched you in vale and glade:
Say, will you dream of our loving shade?"

Dancing and whirling, the little leaves went:
Winter had called them, and they were content.
Soon fast asleep in their earthly beds,
The snow laid a coverlet over their heads.

Answer in complete oral sentences: —

1. How many stanzas are there in this poem?
2. In the first stanza of *The Wind and the Leaves*, who is speaking? In the third stanza?
3. What was the time of year? How do you know?
4. What were the "dresses of red and gold"? At whose bidding did they put them on? What dresses did they lay off?
5. How did the leaves "sing little songs"?
6. Why were the cricket and the leaves "friends"? the leaves and the brook? the leaves and the lambs?
7. How does a brook "sing"? Did you ever hear one?
8. What is a "fleecy fold"? Do lambs "dream"?
9. How had winter "called" the leaves? In what sort of bed did they sleep? Did they ever wake up?
10. Commit the poem to memory.

LESSON LXIX.

COMPOSITION.

(Oral and then Written.)

Divide your composition into two parts: *Leaves in Spring and Summer* and *Leaves in Autumn and Winter.* Follow the order of the questions below.

When do the leaves come out? What is their color? How does it change as summer comes on? Of what use are the leaves to the tree? Of what other uses are they?

When do the leaves put on bright colors? What causes them to do so? How long do their dresses of red and gold last? What happens then? Are the leaves of any further use?

Rules Convenient for Reference.

1. The first word of every sentence should begin with a capital letter.
2. A period should be placed at the end of a complete statement.
3. An interrogation point should be placed at the end of a sentence which asks a question.
4. Every word in proper names should begin with a capital.
5. The names of the days of the week and of the months of the year should begin with capitals.
6. The first word in every line of poetry should begin with a capital.
7. All names applied to God should begin with capitals.

CHAPTER IV.

LESSON LXX.

COMMON NAMES, OR COMMON NOUNS.

Singular and Plural.

In Lesson L., page 45, we spoke of proper, or special, names. There is another kind of name. The word *dog* may be applied to any dog in the world; that is, the name *dog* is *common* to all dogs. Therefore we say that it is a **common name.** For the same reason, the words *book*, *slate*, and *boy* are common names.

A common name must not begin with a capital unless it stands at the beginning of a sentence.

Select the common names from the following list, and tell why they are common: —

floor	Mary	window	pencil	Ralph
stove	apple	Columbus	Webster	orange

Names that mean but one are said to be **singular.**
Names that mean more than one are said to be **plural.**
Door and *pen* are singular; but *doors* and *pens* are plural.

Tell whether the following nouns are singular or plural and why; —

man	horses	child	doors	robins
girl	boys	kite	knives	apple
children	woman	foxes	oxen	mice

LESSON LXXI.

STORY FROM PICTURE.

(Oral.)

Tell what you see in the picture. Who do you think the man is? Where are the kittens? Where were they? How did they get into trouble? Who first found them? Who told the man? How did he tell him? Are the dog and the cat good friends? Why do you think so? What did the man do? Was he kind-hearted? Did anybody thank him? Do you think the kittens learned a lesson?

(Written.)

Write a story from the picture, making it as interesting as you can.

LESSON LXXII

SPELLING EXERCISE ON PLURALS.

Learn to spell the following nouns : —

chimneys	pianos	babies	journeys
knives	potatoes	wives	candies
ponies	valleys	foxes	ladies
children	oxen	women	glasses

Use the *singular* of each noun in an oral sentence.
Change each sentence so that the name shall be *plural*, and note the other changes which you are obliged to make.

LESSON LXXIII.

MEMORY EXERCISE.

Read and commit to memory the following poem: —

THE BROWN THRUSH.

There's a merry brown thrush sitting up in the tree.
He's singing to me! He's singing to me!
And what does he say, little girl, little boy?
"Oh, the world's running over with joy!
    Don't you hear? Don't you see?
    Hush! Look! In my tree,
I'm as happy as happy can be!"

And the brown thrush keeps singing, "A nest do you see,
And five eggs hid by me in the juniper tree?
Don't meddle! don't touch, little girl, little boy,
Or the world will lose some of its joy!
    Now I'm glad! now I'm free!
    And I always shall be,
If you never bring sorrow to me."

So the merry brown thrush sings away in the tree,
To you and to me, to you and to me;
And he sings all the day, little girl, little boy,
"Oh, the world's running over with joy;
But long it won't be,
Don't you know? don't you see?
Unless we're as good as can be."
— Lucy Larcom.

LESSON LXXIV.

PRONUNCIATION.

Pronounce the following words according to the marking: —

ac cĕnt′ ed	băl lōōn′	băl′ us ter
a gainst′ (gĕnst)	bou quet′ (kā)	băl′ us trāde
al′ wāys	cĕl′ lar	cū′ po lâ
ā′ prĭ cŏt	cŏr′ al	grĭ māce′

Tell how many syllables there are in each word, which syllable is accented, and name the vowel sound in each accented syllable.

Use each word in a sentence which shall clearly show that you know its correct meaning.

Most people mispronounce some of the words in the foregoing columns and very few can use them all correctly. Study this lesson very carefully.

LESSON LXXV.

INFORMATION EXERCISE.

(Oral.)

1. Have you ever seen a brickyard?
2. Of what are bricks made?
3. How are they made?

4. What is a brickkiln?
5. What can you say about the color of bricks?
6. What are some of their uses?
7. What is the man called who builds houses of bricks?
8. What is the shape of a brick, and how large are bricks usually made? Measure one.
9. Which do you think are better for the building of houses, bricks or stones? Why?

Possibly some obliging boy may bring to school a brick that has been burned, and one that has not; also a piece of clay from which bricks are made.

LESSON LXXVI.

COMPOSITION.

Write what you have learned about bricks, making use of the questions in Lesson LXXV.

LESSON LXXVII.

THIS, THAT, THESE, THOSE.

The words *this* and *these* refer to what is near; *that* and *those* to what is distant.

Examples: *This* book belongs to me; *that* on your desk belongs to the teacher.
These apples are sweet; *those* yonder are very sour.

This and *that* refer to one thing; *these* and *those* to more than one.

Examples: *This* is a good pen; *those* are very poor.
That was a good story you told yesterday, but *these* in *this* book are too simple.

Exercise.

(Oral and then Written.)

Fill each blank below with one of these words — *this, these, them, that, those :* —

1. What is —— in your hand?
2. —— is a knife.
3. Have you sharpened —— pencils on your desk?
4. Yes, I have sharpened ——, and —— on the teacher's desk.
5. Do you think —— knife is better than —— one?
6. Certainly, and —— pencils are better than —— on your desk.
7. Why are —— better than —— on my desk?
8. —— on your desk are not sharpened at all, while —— are all ready for use.
9. —— will soon be as well sharpened as ——.
10. —— knife and —— pencils will keep you busy for some time.

LESSON LXXVIII.

MEMORY EXERCISE.

Read and commit to memory the following poem: —

GUESS.

I see two lilies, white as snow,
That mother loves and kisses so;
Dearer are they than gold or lands:
Guess me the lilies — Baby's hands!

I know a rosebud fairer far
Than any buds of summer are;
Sweeter than sweet winds of the south:
Guess me the rosebud — Baby's mouth!

I know a place where shines the sun —
Yes, long, long after day is done;

Oh, how it loves to linger there!
Guess me the sunshine — Baby's hair!

There are two windows where I see
My own glad face peep out at me;
These windows beam like June's own skies:
Guess me the riddle — Baby's eyes!

LESSON LXXIX.

POETRY.

Pieces like that in Lesson LXXVIII. are called **poetry**. Each piece is a **poem**.

Each line of poetry is one **verse**. How many verses has each stanza? How many verses has the whole poem? Read one verse in the first stanza. One in the third. Read the last verse in the poem.

Verses are said to **rhyme** when they end with similar sounds. Tell which verses rhyme in each stanza. Why?

Turn to *The Wind and the Leaves* (page 58). Tell the number of stanzas, the number of verses in each, and the verses that rhyme.

LESSON LXXX.

REPRODUCTION.

Read the following story carefully, once or twice. Do not try to remember the sentences, but try to understand them. Then close your book, and think how you would tell the story in your own words without using the word *I*.

If you have an opportunity, tell the story to the class before you write it.

When you write the story, add one paragraph of your own, telling what you think of the bird's act.

True Story of a Fishhawk.

When I was a little girl I lived in Virginia, near the Potomac River. One sunny May morning my father said, "Come, Elinor, I want you to go with me." Of course I was glad to go, and in a few minutes I was on my pony's back. We took the road by the river. The birds were singing merrily, and delicate wild flowers timidly looked out into this great world. As we came near the woods, the air was filled with smoke, and we could see the flames creeping among the dead leaves on the ground.

We stopped our horses and listened. What strange cry was that we heard? It came from a bird above us, flying slowly round and round. What is the trouble? Ah! We can see a tall tree trunk by the roadside. In the topmost branches is a nest, and around it the bird is flying. Her little brood is there.

The flames are even now running up a dead vine that clings to the trunk. Some of the twigs of the nest are on fire. The bird stops her cries, flies swiftly to the nest, and pulls out the burning twigs with her beak. But she cannot pull them out fast enough. Oh, how we wished that we could help her! The little birds must burn. What will the mother bird do? She quietly folds her wings over her little ones, and dies with them.

LESSON LXXXI.

SOUNDS OF CONSONANTS.

The consonants b, d, f, h, j, k, l, m, p, q, r, t, v, w, y, z, are never marked in the dictionary, because they always stand for the same or (in the case of d, as in *chafed*) for nearly the same sounds.

In the word *cent*, the sound of c is soft, or like the sound of s. In *can*, the sound of c is hard, or like the sound of k. The letter is marked thus: —

çent, can.

SOUNDS OF CONSONANTS.

In *gentle*, the sound of *g* is soft, like the sound of *j*. In *get*, the sound of *g* is hard. The letter is marked thus: —

ġentle, g̅et.

In *sun*, the sound of *s* is sharp. When *s* stands for this sound, it is not marked in the dictionary.

In *rising*, *s* has the sound of *z*, and is said to be *vocal*, because the *voice* is heard in the sound. When it stands for this sound, the *s* is marked thus: —

riṣing.

Oral Exercise.

Referring to the list at the beginning of the lesson, give the sounds of the consonants that are never marked.

In which of the following words is the sound of *c* hard, and in which soft?

cellar	cinder	cut
caller	curve	ceiling

How would you mark *c* in each word?

In which of the following words is the sound of *g* hard and in which soft?

go	general	gander
gave	genius	gentle

How would you mark *g* in each word?

In the following words is the sound of *s* sharp or vocal?

this	miss	misers
his	seem	hers
say	sees	sinner

In which words would you mark the *s*? Which words have both the sharp and the vocal sound of *s*?

How would you mark the *c*, *g*, and *s* in each of the following words?

grass	crags	cries
gems	sense	nice
circle	singe	lounge

LESSON LXXXII.

STORY FROM PICTURE.

(Oral and then Written.)

Connect a story with this picture, and arrange your composition in four paragraphs.

SUGGESTIONS.

Robins; season of year; where they have been all winter; they are glad to get back; where is the tree?

Building the nest; lining it; eggs; number and color.

The baby birds; how they look; how long they live in the nest; how they are fed; how they are taught to fly.

Why we should be kind to the birds; the pleasure they give; their happy and useful lives.

LESSON LXXXIII.

MEMORY EXERCISE.

Read and commit to memory the following poem: —

KEEP A WATCH ON YOUR WORDS.

Keep a watch on your words, my darlings,
    For words are wonderful things;
They are sweet like the bees' fresh honey;
    Like the bees, they have terrible stings.
They can bless like the warm, glad sunshine,
    And brighten a lonely life;
They can cut, in the strife of anger,
    Like a cruel two-edged knife.

Let them pass through your lips unchallenged,
    If their errand is true and kind,
If they come to support the weary,
    To comfort and help the blind.
If a bitter, revengeful spirit
    Prompts the words, let them be unsaid.
They may flash through a brain like lightning,
    Or fall on a heart like lead.

Keep them back, if they're cold and cruel,
    Under bar and lock and seal;
The wounds they make, my darlings,
    Are always slow to heal.
May peace guard your lives, and ever,
    From this time of your early youth,
May the words that you daily utter
    Be the beautiful words of truth.

Write the thoughts of this poem in your own words, and tell what you think of them.

LESSON LXXXIV.

COMPOSITION.

Write the following story as though there were two squirrels instead of one, and use *we* instead of *I*:—

The Squirrel.

A little red squirrel lives in a tree near our home, and we are getting to be quite good friends.

When I first saw him, he was on a limb of a tree just over my head; and what a noise he did make! I think he was trying to tell me to go away.

I put two or three nuts on the ground near the tree, and he soon came and picked them up. You ought to have seen how funny he looked with two large nuts in his mouth.

The next day I went and left some more nuts in the same place, and he came and picked them up while I was standing near by. In a few days he would come and take the nuts from my hand, jump upon my shoulder, and then leap into the tree.

Now, when I go near his tree, I find him watching for me. He will run to meet me, jump into my arms, and look into all my pockets for something to eat.

LESSON LXXXV.

INFORMATION LESSON.

INSECTS.

Insects wear their skeletons on the outside; while birds, snakes, and fishes carry their skeletons inside their bodies. The insect has no real bones; but it has a head, a chest, and a body, each protected by a case and connected with the other parts by a movable joint. Joined to the chest it has six legs, and usually four wings.

The mouth of an insect contains jaws that work toward each other horizontally, instead of up and down as in the dog or horse. Some of them, like the cockroach and grasshopper, have jaws for crushing and chewing. The mouth of others, like the butterfly, that sucks sweet juices from flowers, has softer jaws. The under lip is turned into a tube, which, in some, rolls, and, when unrolled, is long enough to reach the calyx of a deep flower. From the sides of the mouth run out long feelers which carry the sense of touch, though insects have some power of feeling in their lips and feet.

For breathing, the insect has holes nearly all over the body; and tubes connect these holes with the living organs within.

But the most wonderful thing of all about them is the change of form through which they pass. First in the egg; then the living thing that is hatched from the egg, which is called the larva, or caterpillar; then the chrysalis, in which the larva is wrapped up like a baby in a blanket; and last, out of the chrysalis, the perfect insect.

Like birds, insects live in the air, the earth, and the water.

—JOHONNOT's "Flyers, Creepers, and Swimmers."

TOPICS FOR CONVERSATION.

What can you tell about the bones of insects? How does the mouth of an insect differ from the mouth of a dog or a horse? What have you learned about the mouth of a grasshopper? of a butterfly? What are the feelers?

What can you say of the breathing apparatus of an insect?

Through what changes in form does an insect pass? What insect, if any, have you observed while it was thus changing?

Name some insect that lives in the air; in the water.

LESSON LXXXVI.

COMPOSITION.

Write what you have learned about insects.

LESSON LXXXVII.

POSSESSIVES.

All names, common or proper, when singular, are made to show ownership by adding the apostrophe and *s*: —

Examples: *Alice's* hat blew into the ditch.
The *horse's* head is very long.

Names that show ownership are called possessives.

Exercise.

Write each of the following names in a sentence so as to denote ownership: —

fox	mouse	horse	Mr. Smith
Ned	Harry	Charles	Miss Gray
puss	Fido	woman	Uncle George
fish	tiger	James	Mrs. Bliss
ass	rabbit	walrus	Dr. Davis

In your sentences, which words are possessives?
Tell in each case what is possessed.

REPRODUCTION.

LESSON LXXXVIII.

POSSESSIVES (*continued*).

Plural nouns that do not end with *s* denote ownership by adding the apostrophe and *s* ('*s*); as, *men's hats*.

Exercise I.

Write in a sentence each of the following plural nouns so as to express ownership, or possession: —

men　　geese　　women　　mice　　oxen　　children

Plural nouns ending in *s* denote ownership by adding the apostrophe; as, *boys' hats, girls' dresses*.

Exercise 2.

Use in a sentence each of the following plural nouns so as to express ownership: —

horses	camels	canaries	ladies
lions	girls	monkeys	robins
robins	eagles	rabbits	cows

Point out the possessive in each sentence, and tell what is possessed.

LESSON LXXXIX.

REPRODUCTION.

Reproduce orally the following story: —

THE OLD HORSE'S APPEAL.

Once upon a time, a king who wished justice to be done to all his people, had a bell put up, so that any one who was injured by another might ring it. Whenever it was rung, the king called together a council of the wise men to decide what should be done. From long use, the lower end of the rope was worn away, and a piece of wild vine was fastened on, to lengthen it.

It so happened that a knight had a noble horse, which had served him long and well, but, having grown old and useless, was meanly and cruelly turned out on the common to take care of himself. Driven by hunger, the horse began biting at the vine, when the bell rang loud and clear.

The wise men came, and finding that it was a poor, half-starved horse that was asking for justice, looked into his case, and decided that the knight whom he had served in his youth should feed and care for him in his old age. And the king made the decree, adding to it a heavy fine if the knight did not do his duty to the faithful animal.

To THE TEACHER.—Have the pupils read Longfellow's poem called *The Bell of Atri*.

LESSON XC.

STUDY OF POEM.

BOYS WANTED.

Boys of spirit, boys of will,
  Boys of muscle, brain, and power,
Fit to cope with anything,—
  These are wanted every hour.

Not the weak and whining drones
  Who all troubles magnify,—
Not the watchword of "I can't,"
  But the nobler one, "I'll try."

Do whate'er you have to do,
  With a true and earnest zeal;
Bend your sinews to the task,—
  "Put your shoulders to the wheel."

Though your duty may be hard,
  Look not on it as an ill;
If it be an honest task,
  Do it with an honest will.

STUDY OF POEM. 77

> In the workshop, on the farm,
> Or wherever you may be,
> From your future efforts, boys,
> Comes a nation's destiny.

Exercise.

(Oral.)

1. Give a description of the boys, and tell what is meant.
2. What does the third verse in the first stanza mean?
3. "These are wanted every hour" where and by whom?
4. What is meant by "whining drones"?
5. What is it to "magnify" troubles? What is the opposite?
6. What is a "watchword"?
7. What are "your sinews"?
8. "Put your shoulder" to what wheel? Why your *shoulder?*
9. Give your thought of the fourth stanza.
10. Is the boy in the workshop as good as any other?
11. Which would you prefer, to have nothing to do, or to earn your own bread?
12. What do the last two lines mean? Do you believe what they say?
13. What *nation* is meant?
14. Do the boys spoken of in the poem mean the boys in this very school?
15. Do you love your country? What is a patriot?
16. Do you love to read about patriots?
17. How can every boy make his country better and stronger?
18. Can you name one boy who will try to do it?

CHAPTER V.

LESSON XCI.

DICTATION EXERCISE.

Willie's First Visit to the Farm.

One pleasant evening in July, Willie arrived at his uncle's farm. He was tired out by a long day's journey, and soon went to bed. The next morning he fed Aunt Lizzie's hens and chickens. He found three hens' nests in the haymow. After dinner he drove his uncle's horse to the post office. On the way home he called at Cousin George's store and bought some tea, coffee, and sugar.

Point out the common nouns and the proper nouns. Which of these nouns denote ownership?

LESSON XCII.

INFORMATION LESSON.

A caterpillar is hatched from a tiny egg, and is at first very small. It grows fast because it eats so many green leaves. In the course of  a few weeks, it sheds its skin several times. When it is full-grown, it stops eating and looks about for a place where it can be undisturbed.

Different kinds of caterpillars choose different kinds of places. Those that become butterflies generally fasten themselves to twigs, or to some other surface, by silk threads. At the end of one or two days, the skin of the caterpillar splits and falls off.

Its body is then of an entirely different shape and color, and is called a chrysalis. After several days or several weeks, the skin of the chrysalis splits, and the butterfly comes out. Its wings are crumpled and moist, but they soon dry in the air, and the butterfly spreads them and flies away.

Some of the caterpillars which become moths crawl into the earth and there change to chrysalides. Others spin silk cocoons on twigs or fences or rocks, and change to chrysalides inside these.

Butterflies and moths do not grow after they come from the chrysalides. They lay eggs which produce little caterpillars. Sometimes one butterfly or moth will lay more than two hundred eggs.

— H. L. Clapp.

Topics for Study and Conversation.

Eggs — where they may be found. Food of caterpillars. The skin. The chrysalis. The changes that take place from the egg to the butterfly. Differences between the butterfly and the moth.

LESSON XCIII.

COMPOSITION.

Write what you have learned about Caterpillars.

LESSON XCIV.

I, ME, HE, HIM, SHE, HER.

Exercise.

(Oral and then Written.)

Fill each blank below with *I, me, he, him, she,* or *her.*

1. The dog chased Willie and ——.
2. Willie and —— ran into the house.
3. Between you and ——, this is a hard lesson.
4. The trouble all came between —— and ——.
5. The teacher thought it was ——, but both —— and —— told her that it was not so.
6. Mother told Ned and —— to go to the post office.

LESSON XCV.

REVIEW.

(Oral and then Written.)

Make a statement beginning with *There is;* one beginning with *There are.*

Make the same statements without using the word *there.*

Ask a question beginning with *Are you;* one beginning with *Were you.* Change the questions to statements.

Make a statement beginning with *There was;* one beginning with *There were.* Change the statements to questions.

Make the same statements without using *there.*

Ask a question beginning with *Is there;* one beginning with *Are there.*

Make a statement beginning with *You are;* one beginning with *You were.*

Ask a question beginning with *Was there;* one beginning with *Were there.*

LESSON XCVI.

STORY FROM PICTURE.

TOPICS FOR STUDY AND CONVERSATION.

Scene of picture. Father and son. Where are they going? Why do you think it a large boat?

What interests the boy? What do you know about a whale, its size, its life, its capture, and its uses to man? The birds. Why do they hover around the ship?

Length of this voyage. Why would you like such a trip?

Tell a story about *Jamie's Vacation*.

LESSON XCVII.

MEMORY EXERCISE.

Commit to memory and recite the following poem: —

The Little People.

A dreary place would be this earth,
　Were there no little people in it;
The song of life would lose its mirth,
　Were there no children to begin it;

No little forms like buds to grow,
　And make the admiring heart surrender;
No little hands on breast and brow,
　To keep the thrilling love chords tender.

The sterner soul would grow more stern,
　Unfeeling nature more inhuman;
And man to Stoic coldness turn,
　And woman would be less than woman.

Life's song, indeed, would lose its charm,
　Were there no babies to begin it;
A doleful place this world would be,
　Were there no little people in it.

LESSON XCVIII.

REPRODUCTION.

(Oral and then Written.)

Read the following fable, and then write it in your own words: —

The Goose and the Golden Eggs.

Once upon a time there was a man who had a goose he thought a great deal of. And well he might do so, for this was the strangest goose that ever lived. Every day she laid an egg. "There is nothing strange about that," you will say. Ah! but the eggs this goose laid were of solid gold. Think of that!

IS AND ARE.

Day after day this strange bird laid a shining golden egg for her master. That was why he liked the goose so much. You may be sure he did not sell these eggs in the market. Not he: he hid them away carefully in a great iron box.

Every day he found a bright new golden egg in the goose's nest, and added it to the pile. He was so glad to get it that he could hardly wait for the night to pass and the morning to come. Each day seemed as long as a week to him.

When he saw the pile growing higher and higher in the iron box, he rubbed his hands with glee. "Ah!" said he to himself, "if it were only full, I should be the richest man in the world."

He could think of nothing but his golden pile. At last he grew so greedy that he wanted all his gold at once. He thought he would find plenty of eggs in the goose's body, and not have to wait and wait and wait any longer.

So one day he killed the wonderful bird. But when he came to look for more eggs, — why, there were none to be found!

Foolish man! He had killed the goose that laid the golden eggs.

LESSON XCIX.

IS AND ARE.

Exercise.

(Oral and then Written.)

Fill the blanks below with *is* or *are*, and give reasons for your choice. Then fill them with *was* or *were*.

1. All of the chickens —— out of the coop.
2. Not one of the chickens —— out of the coop.
3. Both of the horses —— lame.
4. Neither of the horses —— lame.
5. John and Mary —— going to the party.
6. John or Mary —— going to the party.
7. All of the girls —— at school.
8. Every one of the girls —— at school.
9. All of the children —— to receive books.
10. Each of the children —— to receive a book.

LESSON C.

SINGULARS AND PLURALS.

Review Exercise.

(Oral and then Written.)

In the following sentences, use plural nouns instead of the nouns in Italics, and make such other changes as are necessary: —

1. The *bird* carries straws in its *mouth* to build its nest.
2. It builds its *nest* in a tall tree.
3. There is a *nest* in a *tree* near our house.
4. There is a blue *egg* in this nest.
5. The *egg* has black spots on it.
6. A little *boy* knows where the *bird* has its *nest*.
7. Do you think this *boy* will harm the *nest*? Not he!
8. He watched the *bird* while it was building its *nest*.
9. He likes to hear it sing its sweet *song*.
10. The *boy* thinks a *bird* has as good a right to live and be happy as a *boy* has.
11. He calls any *boy* who will harm a bird's *nest* a *coward*.

LESSON CI.

PRONUNCIATION EXERCISE.

Pronounce the following words as marked: —

for bāde'	gĕn'tle man	ī dē'a
ĕn'gīne	hăl lōō'	in stĕad'
drowned	height	I tăl'ics
drown'ing	ho ri'zon	noth'ing ($o = \breve{u}$)

After studying the foregoing words, copy them upon your slate, then close your book and mark each word to denote its proper pronunciation.

Use each word in an oral sentence.

LESSON CII.

STORY FROM PICTURE.

(Oral.)

SUGGESTIONS.

Name of boy. The city in which he lived. Had been at school — after school. Appearance of street. Old lady — poor — bundle — hard work — difficulty in crossing the street. What the boy did. Kindness to the poor — respect for age.

(Written.)

Write a story about *A Noble Boy*, using these suggestions.

LESSON CIII.

PARAGRAPHS.

For convenience, books are divided into chapters, and **chapters** are divided into **paragraphs**. Each paragraph relates to some particular part of the subject upon which the author is writing. Thus, the first five lines of this lesson form a paragraph.

The first word of a paragraph is usually set in, or indented, to the right of the first words in the lines above and below it.

It would be much more difficult to read books if they were not divided into chapters and paragraphs. This you will easily understand if you try to read some one's composition that has not been divided into paragraphs.

A paragraph should contain all that relates to some particular part of a topic. If you examine the paragraphs in any carefully written book, you can tell what the author is writing about in each one.

There are usually two or more sentences in a paragraph, but it may contain only one. It must be remembered that all the sentences in a paragraph should express thoughts which are closely related to each other.

Answer in oral sentences: —

How many paragraphs are there above this question? How many lines are indented? What is the first paragraph about? the second? the third? the fourth? the fifth?

Why should letters and other kinds of composition be divided into paragraphs? How can you tell when to begin a new paragraph?

LESSON CIV.

INFORMATION LESSON.

SPIDERS.

Spiders are not insects. Most people think that a spider is an insect; but they are quite wrong.

An insect looks as if its body were almost cut into three parts; and it always has six legs. Now, the body of the spider is made up of two pieces joined together. Then the spider has eight legs instead of six—four on each side.

If you could look inside the body of a spider, you would see that it does not breathe as insects do. All insects breathe through little tubes that run all over the body, and open into a row of holes along each side. But the spider has a sort of lung, and does not have the air tubes.

Insects always go through a number of changes after they are hatched; but the spider has no such changes. A young spider is of the same shape as an old one. So, you see that spiders are not insects.

All spiders spin webs of some sort through all their lives; while no insect can spin a web of any kind after it has passed through its second change. The silkworm can spin; but when the silkworm becomes a moth, it can spin no more.

There are a great many sorts of spiders,

such as wolf spiders, hunting spiders, mason spiders, field spiders, etc. (See Wood's "Natural History Readers," and Johonnot's "Flyers, Creepers, and Swimmers.")

TOPICS FOR STUDY AND CONVERSATION.

Not a true insect. Why? Body divided into two parts. Number of legs. How it breathes. Insects go through what changes? Webs, — how made.

Different kinds of spiders — wolf spiders — hunting spiders — mason spiders — field spiders — water spiders.

How water spiders build their nests. How garden spiders spin their webs. How they catch their prey.

LESSON CV.

COMPOSITION.

Write a composition on *The Spider* following the order of the Suggestions in Lesson CIV., and dividing your composition into three paragraphs. It is not necessary that you write on every topic under the suggestions. You may select from each group.

LESSON CVI.

THE APOSTROPHE.

Sometimes a letter is omitted in writing a word, or two words are joined together with one or more letters omitted. The new words thus formed are called **contractions**; as, *o'er, don't.*

In contractions, the apostrophe is used to take the place of omitted letters. Contractions should be used sparingly.

DICTATION.

Copy the following contractions, and write after each the word or words in full.

it's ——	I'll ——	hadn't ——
can't ——	won't ——	I'm ——
I've ——	o'er ——	wouldn't ——
don't ——	didn't ——	he'll ——
doesn't ——	there's ——	'twas ——
we'll ——	e'er ——	ma'am ——

Name the letter or letters omitted in each contraction.

What difference can you see between contractions and abbreviations?

Remember that the apostrophe is a necessary part of every written contraction.

LESSON CVII.

DICTATION.

Write from dictation the following questions: —

1. On what day is (or was) Easter Sunday this year?
2. What occurs the first Monday of every December?
3. What takes place every fourth year, on the first Tuesday after the first Monday in November?
4. What usually comes on the last Thursday of November?
5. What is the Friday before Easter called?
6. Can there be five Saturdays in February? Explain.
7. On what day of the week was (or will be) the Fourth of July this year?
8. What month, or months, will have five Sundays this year?
9. How many of the days of the week have names that are dissyllables?

Write answers to the foregoing questions. Use complete sentences.

LESSON CVIII.

STUDY OF POEM.

THE THREE BELLS.

Beneath the low-hung night cloud
    That raked her splintering mast,
The good ship settled slowly;
    The cruel leak gained fast.

Over the awful ocean
    Her signal guns pealed out.
Dear God! was that thy answer
    From the horror round about?

A voice came down the wild wind,
    "Ho! ship ahoy!" its cry:
"Our stout Three Bells of Glasgow
    Shall lay till daylight by."

Hour after hour crept slowly,
    Yet on the heaving swells
Tossed up and down the ship-lights,
    The lights of The Three Bells.

And ship to ship made signals,
    Man answered back to man,
While oft, to cheer and hearten,
    The Three Bells nearer ran;

And the captain from her taffrail,
    Sent down his hopeful cry:
"Take heart! hold on!" he shouted,
    "The Three Bells shall lay by!"

All night across the waters
    The tossing lights shone clear;
All night from reeling taffrail
    The Three Bells sent her cheer.

And when the dreary watches
Of storm and darkness passed,
Just as the wreck lurched under,
All souls were saved at last.

Sail on, Three Bells, forever,
In grateful memory sail!
Ring on, Three Bells of rescue,
Above the wave and gale!

Type of the Love eternal,
Repeat the Master's cry,
As tossing through our darkness
The lights of God draw nigh.
—JOHN G. WHITTIER.

Oral Exercise.

1. How many ships are spoken of in the poem, *The Three Bells*? Tell something about each of them.
2. What are "signal guns"? In the third and fourth verses of the second stanza, what does the question mean?
3. Whose voice "came down the wild wind"? What did it say? Why does the poet say, "Shall *lay* by"?[1] Did you ever see any "ship-lights"? What are they?
4. Give the meaning of the fifth stanza. Of the sixth. What is a "taffrail"? Why does the poet say "reeling taffrail"? What is meant by "sent her cheer"?

LESSON CIX.

COMPOSITION.

Write the story of *The Three Bells*.

[1] A private note from the poet to the author says, "An old salt would hardly know what was meant by the expression, 'shall *lie* by.'"

CHAPTER VI.

LESSON CX.

LETTER WRITING.

A letter is a kind of composition, and it should always be carefully written. The **form** of a letter is of great importance, especially as regards the first and the last part of it.

A letter is made up of four parts: the **heading**, the **salutation**, the **body** of the letter, and the **conclusion**. Another matter of great importance is the **address** on the envelope, or the **superscription**.

Notice carefully the arrangement, the capital letters, and the marks of punctuation in the following letter, and then copy it.

HEADING.

Waltham, Mass., Dec. 11, 1893.

SALUTATION.

My dear Mother,

BODY OF LETTER.

I arrived safe and on time. The journey did not seem long, as I was much interested in watching the strange country through which we passed.

THE HEADING.

Aunt Amy met me at the station, and in a few minutes we were chatting merrily over a good warm supper.

CONCLUSION.

Your loving daughter,
Jennie.

LESSON CXI.

THE HEADING.

The **heading** of a letter should indicate the place where, and the time when, the letter was written. When answering a letter, a person looks to the heading to see how to direct his answer.

In the letter in Lesson CX., *Waltham, Mass.*, tells where the letter was written, and *Dec. 11, 1893*, tells when it was written. If this letter had been written in a large city, the **number** and **street** should also have been given in the heading.

Study carefully the arrangement, capitals, and punctuation of the following headings:—

Scranton, R. I., Nov. 7, 1892.

Winchester, Middlesex Co., Mass.,
Tuesday, March 13, 1890.

Cook Co. Normal School,
Englewood, Illinois,
April 15, 1891.

149 Wabash Ave., Chicago, Ill.,
March 21, 1891.

LESSON CXII.

THE HEADING (continued).

Oral Exercise.

Of what should the heading of a letter consist?
What is the use of the heading?
What items should be contained in the heading of a letter that is written in a village?
What additional items should be contained in the heading of a letter written in a large city? Why?
Tell what marks of punctuation you would use in the heading.

Written Exercise.

Write the following headings, taking care to arrange and punctuate them correctly: —

1. New York, Auburn, Jan. 4, 1890.
2. June 16, 1891, Mass., Boston, 47 Exeter St.
3. Chicago, Ill., Palmer House, 1893, April 14.
4. Columbia, S.C., April 19, 1890, Laurel St., No. 84.

What heading would you use, if writing a letter from your own home?

LESSON CXIII.

THE SALUTATION.

The **salutation** is the term of politeness, respect, or affection, with which we introduce a letter.

In letters to dear friends, salutations like the following are used: —

My dear Mother.   Dear Uncle.
My dear Henry.   Dear Miss Johnson.

THE SALUTATION. 95

Copy the following forms, and notice carefully the position, capitals, and punctuation of the headings and salutations: —

        Charleston, S.C., Aug. 8, 1893.
My dear Mother,
 I am very glad to hear, etc.

        Englewood, Ill., April 15, 1894.
Dear Uncle,
 My father has been very sick, etc.

        Jacksonville, Fla., Sept. 12, 1892.
Dear Miss Johnson,
 You must have heard, etc.

In letters to strangers or to very slight acquaintances, the following forms of salutation are used: —

Mr. Robert James,   Mrs. Addison Ray,
 Dear Sir,   Dear Madam,

Jerome Bates, Esq.,   Miss Emma James,
 Dear Sir,   Dear Madam,

The salutation should in general be followed by a comma, as in the examples given; or, if the letter begins on the same line, by a comma and a dash; as, —

Rev. Thos. H. Wilson,
 Dear Sir, — I am pleased to learn, etc.

Write the foregoing salutations as your teacher dictates them.

LESSON CXIV.

THE SALUTATION (*continued*).

Oral Exercise.

What would be the salutation, if you were writing a letter to your mother? father? brother? sister? a schoolmate? a friend? a gentleman whom you had met only once or twice? an unmarried lady who is an intimate friend? a married lady who is a slight acquaintance?

Written Exercise.

1. Write the heading and salutation of a letter to your mother, from Albany, March 7, 1880.
2. To your brother, from Scranton, Pa., April 4, 1879.
3. To a gentleman and near friend, from Chicago, Ill., 486 Wabash Avenue, Jan. 8, 1875.
4. To your teacher, from your own home to-day.
5. To a schoolmate, from Washington, D.C., 54 H St., Jan. 1, 1884.
6. To a stranger from whom you wish to obtain employment.

LESSON CXV.

THE CONCLUSION.

The **conclusion** of a letter is that which is added after the body of the letter is finished. It consists of the **complimentary close** and the **signature**.

The **complimentary close**, consisting of words of respect or affection, is written on the line below the body of the letter. If long, it may occupy two, or even more, lines.

The **signature** is written on the line next below the complimentary close.

Be careful that neither is crowded too far toward the right-hand edge of the paper.

CONCLUSIONS.

Your loving daughter,
Jennie.

Yours respectfully,
M. J. Cherrington.

ORAL REVIEW. 97

Yours truly,
Robert Richmond.

Your affectionate nephew,
James Bradley.

Sincerely your friend,
Allen Thornton.

LESSON CXVI.

ORAL REVIEW.

1. What does the *conclusion* of a letter include?
2. What is meant by the *complimentary close*? by the *signature*? by the *salutation*?
3. What would be a proper *complimentary close* of a letter to your father? mother? brother? sister? friend?
4. Where should the *signature* be written? the *salutation*? the *complimentary close*?
5. What items should appear in the *heading* of a letter?
6. How should the heading be punctuated?
7. What is the difference between the heading of a letter written in a village and that of one written in a city?
8. Describe the *salutation* and the *conclusion* of a letter written to your father, giving capitals and punctuation.
9. Describe the *exact position* of the different parts of the heading, the address, and the conclusion.
10. To whom would the following salutations be appropriate?

Mr. James Ritchie,
 Dear Sir,

Mrs. Louise Chandler,
 Dear Madam,

My dear Son,

American Book Company,
 Gentlemen,

Supt. M. J. Brown,
 Dear Sir,

Dear Arthur,

LESSON CXVII.

MEMORY EXERCISE.

Commit the following poem to memory : —

THE WILL AND THE WAY.

There's something I'd have you remember, boys,
   To help in the battle of life;
It will give you strength in the time of need
   And help in the hour of strife.
Whenever there's something that should be done,
   Don't be a coward, and say,
"What use to try?" Remember, then,
   That "where there's a will there's a way."

There's many a failure for those who win;
   But though at first they fail,
They try again, and the earnest ones
   Are sure at last to prevail.
Though the mountain is steep and hard to climb,
   You can win the heights I say,
If you make up your mind to reach the top,
   For "where there's a will there's a way."

The men who stand at the top are those
   Who never could bear defeat;
Their failures only made them strong
   For the work they had to meet.
The will to do and the will to dare
   Is what we want to-day;
What has been done can be done again,
   For the will finds out the way.

1. What is the thing to remember? Why?
2. Give the meaning of the first four lines of second stanza.
3. What is meant by "the mountain?"
4. How can failures make men strong?

LESSON CXVIII.

A LETTER.

Write to your teacher a letter of three paragraphs about the events of yesterday. Show that you can write a correct heading, salutation, and conclusion. Be very careful of the language in the body of your letter.

LESSON CXIX.

THE ENVELOPE.

Turn to Lesson CX., and you will find a letter from Jennie to her mother. Before this letter is posted, it must be folded and placed in an envelope, which should be properly directed in order that it may promptly reach its destination. We will suppose that Jennie's father is living in Greytown, Pa., and that his name is Philip C. Murray. Jennie should direct the letter as follows: —

Mrs. Philip C. Murray,

  Greytown,

    Pa.

[Stamp.]

THE ENVELOPE.

If Mrs. Murray's address were in a large city like Philadelphia, the street and number should be added to the address on the envelope, as follows: —

```
┌─────────────────────────────────────────────┐
│                                    ┌──────┐ │
│                                    │Stamp.│ │
│                                    └──────┘ │
│                                             │
│     Mrs. Philip C. Murray,                  │
│          1016 Chestnut Street,              │
│                    Philadelphia,            │
│                         Pa.                 │
│                                             │
└─────────────────────────────────────────────┘
```

The width of an envelope is usually a very little more than one half the length. Sometimes it requires the folding of the paper into two parts and sometimes into three.

Written Exercise.

Draw five rectangles representing five envelopes. Direct them to the following persons, noticing carefully the distance of each part of the address from the left end of the envelope: —

1. To your teacher at her own home.
2. To your father or mother.
3. To Mrs. Jas. R. Munroe, who resides at 47 High St., Providence, R.I.
4. To Mr. C. R. Stetson, who is a clergyman living in Bloomington, Ill.
5. To George E. Davis, at 1896 Lake St., Chicago, Ill.

A LETTER.

LESSON CXX.

STORY FROM PICTURE.

SUGGESTIONS.

The names of the children. Christmas time in their home. People to whom Christmas brings little happiness. How the children came to think of others. Their visit, what they found, and what they did. Why we should remember the poor, especially at Christmas time.

LESSON CXXI.

A LETTER.

John Harrison, of San Francisco, writes to his friend, Walter Manning, of Chicago, March 1, 1894.

The following is an analysis of his letter. Make as many paragraphs as there are topics.

Analysis.

The weather for the past month. His father has been very sick. He has a small garden of his own, and tells what he has planted. He tells how he takes care of his plants, and how they are thriving. He asks Walter to visit him, and describes the route by which he must go. He plans how they will spend their time if Walter should come.

Write the letter in full. Draw and address the envelope.

LESSON CXXII.

ABBREVIATIONS.

Some words are shortened in writing, — two or three letters only representing the whole word; as, *Col.* for *Colonel;* *Esq.* for *Esquire;* *Hon.* for *Honorable,* and *Rev.* for *Reverend.* *Col., Esq., Hon.,* and *Rev.* are called **abbreviations.**

Written Exercise.

Learn the following abbreviations, and use them in sentences: —

@, *at.*	Jas., *James.*
A.M. (*Ante Meridiem*), *Before noon.*	Jno., *John.*
Av., or Ave., *Avenue.*	M. (*Meridian*), *Noon.*
Capt., *Captain.*	Mrs., *Mistress.*
Col., *Colonel.*	N. Y., *New York.*
cts., *cents.*	P.M. (*Post Meridiem*), *Afternoon.*
cwt., *hundredweight.*	P.M., *Postmaster.*
doz., *dozen.*	P.O., *Post Office.*
Esq., *Esquire.*	P.S., *Postscript.*
etc. (*et cætera*), *and so forth.*	Rev., *Reverend.*
Gen., *General.*	St., *Street.*

ABBREVIATIONS.

LESSON CXXIII.

ABBREVIATIONS (*continued*).

Dictation Exercise.

1. Gen. U. S. Grant died July 23, 1885.
2. The morning session of school begins at 9 o'clock A.M. and closes at 12 M.
3. Col. James A. Dean was seen on Lincoln Av., at 2 o'clock P.M.
4. Capt. and Mrs. Barry are living at 312 Arlington St.
5. Rev. H. W. Beecher died March 8, 1887.
6. Samuel Weller added a postscript to his letter, and then took it to the post office.
7. 6 doz. eggs @ 12 cts. a doz. will cost 72 cts.
8. A *company* of soldiers is commanded by a captain; a *regiment*, by a colonel; and an *army*, by a general.
9. Benjamin Disraeli was created a peer for eminent services, with the title of Earl Beaconsfield.
10. Troy weight is used in weighing gold, silver, etc.
11. Rev. M. J. Savage will preach at 4 P.M.

Oral Exercise.

What titles are used in the dictation exercise in connection with the names of persons? What titles are not so used? What titles are abbreviated in the sentences which you have written? What titles are not abbreviated? What titles begin with capital letters? What titles do not begin with capital letters? Make a rule for the use of capitals in titles.

What initials are used as abbreviations? Should such initials be capitals? What mark should be placed after every abbreviation?

What is a postscript? What is the abbreviation for "*and so forth*"? What was the highest office held by Gen. U. S. Grant?

LESSON CXXIV.

REPRODUCTION.

Read the following poem, and tell the story in your own words: —

The Afternoon Nap.

The farmer sat in his easy-chair,
　Smoking his pipe of clay,
While his hale old wife, with busy care,
　Was clearing the dinner away;
A sweet little girl with fine blue eyes,
On her grandfather's knee was catching flies.

The old man laid his hand on her head,
　With a tear on his wrinkled face;
He thought how often, her mother, dead —
　Had sat in the self-same place;
And the tear stole down from his half-shut eye;
"Don't smoke!" said the child, "how it makes you cry!"

The house-dog lay stretched out on the floor,
　Where the shade, after noon, used to steal;
The busy old wife, by the open door,
　Was turning the spinning wheel;
And the old brass clock on the manteltree,
Had plodded along to almost three.

Still the farmer sat in his easy-chair,
　While close to his heaving breast,
The moistened brow and the cheek so fair
　Of his sweet grandchild were pressed;
His head bent down on her soft hair lay;
Fast asleep were they both, that summer day.

(Oral.)

Describe the picture in your imagination of the farm-house, the farmer, his wife, the little girl, and the dog.

LESSON CXXV.

THE BLACKSMITH.

Oral Exercise.

Do you know of any blacksmith's shop near your home? If so, will you visit it with some friend older than yourself?

Keep your eyes wide open while you are in the shop; and then, when you return to school, tell the class all that you have learned about the following things: —

1. Introduction. — Different kinds of smiths. — Business of the blacksmith.
2. Materials used.
3. Names of the tools.
4. Uses of the tools.
5. Forge and bellows.
6. The anvil.
7. Kinds of work done.

LESSON CXXVI.

PRONUNCIATION.

Oral Exercise.

Pronounce the following words according to the marking: —

läugh'ter	prŏb'a bly	shriēked
lēi'ṣure	rē'al ly	sĭt'ting
nĕsts	rĕg'ū lar	sĭxth
pĭc'tūre	rĭ dĭc'ū loŭs	stămped

In the first word what sound has *gh*?
Give the vowel sound in each accented syllable.
Give the vowel sound in each monosyllable.
Give all the vowel sounds in the polysyllable.
Pronounce the two shortest words very distinctly.
Show that you know the meaning of each word, by using it in a sentence.

LESSON CXXVII.

A LETTER.

Suppose a letter to have been written by Walter Manning, of Chicago, Ill., in reply to John Harrison, of San Francisco, Cal. It was dated June 1, 1893.

SUGGESTIONS.

Walter is glad to hear from John. Health of himself and the rest of the family. He has a good boat, which he describes. Sailing party on the Lake, — no accident except the loss of one or two hats. Would be pleased to visit John, — gives reason why he cannot do so this summer.

Write the letter in full. Draw and direct the envelope.

LESSON CXXVIII.

REPRODUCTION.

Read carefully the following story, and write the thoughts in your own words without referring to the book. Divide your story into three paragraphs.

Learn the saying of Horace Mann, and write it word for word at the end of your story. If you know exactly what the saying means, you will never forget it.

THE FORCE OF HABIT.

There was once a horse that used to pull around a sweep which lifted dirt from the depths of the earth. He was kept at the business for nearly twenty years, until he became old, blind, and too stiff in the joints for further use. So he was turned into a pasture, and left to crop the grass without any one to disturb or bother him.

The funny thing about the old horse was that every morning, after grazing awhile, he would start on a tramp, going round and round in a circle, just as he had been accustomed to do for so many years. He would keep it up for hours, and people often stopped to look, and wondered what had got into the head of the venerable animal to make him walk around in such a solemn way when there was no earthly need of it. It was the force of habit.

The boy who forms bad or good habits in his youth will be led by them when he becomes old, and will be miserable or happy accordingly.

Habit is a cable, — we weave a thread of it each day, and at last we cannot break it. — HORACE MANN.

LESSON CXXIX.

STUDY OF POEM.

Read and commit to memory the following poem: —

THE FIRST SNOW FALL.

The snow had begun in the gloaming,
   And busily all the night
Had been heaping field and highway
   With a silence deep and white.

Every pine and fir and hemlock
   Wore ermine too dear for an earl,
And the poorest twig on the elm tree
   Was ridged inch deep with pearl.

. . . .

I stood and watched by the window
   The noiseless work of the sky,
And the sudden flurries of snowbirds,
   Like brown leaves whirling by.

I thought of a mound in sweet Auburn
   Where a little headstone stood;
How the flakes were folding it gently,
   As did robins the babes in the wood.

Up spoke our own little Mabel,
  Saying, "Father, who makes it snow?"
And I told of the good All-Father
  Who cares for us here below.

. . . .

Then, with eyes that saw not, I kissed her;
  And she, kissing back, could not know
That *my* kiss was given to her sister,
  Folded close under deepening snow.

—James Russell Lowell.

TOPICS FOR STUDY AND CONVERSATION.

1. At what time in the day did it begin to snow? How do you know? At what time was Mr. Lowell speaking? How did he know that the snow had been busy all the night? What is the meaning of the last verse in the first stanza?

2. What is ermine? What is its color? Why should it be costly? What is an earl? What is the meaning of the last verse in the second stanza? Describe the picture that this stanza brings to your mind.

3. What two things was the poet watching from his window? What was he thinking about? Where is "sweet Auburn"? Tell the story of *The Babes in the Wood*.

4. Who was watching the snow with the poet? What is meant by "All-Father"? By "eyes that saw not"? Tell the meaning of the sixth stanza.

LESSON CXXX.

REPRODUCTION.

Write in your own words the meaning of the poem entitled *The First Snow Fall*.

CHAPTER VII.

LESSON CXXXI.

DIRECT QUOTATIONS.

Exercise.

(Oral and then Written.)

Copy the following sentences just as they are written: —

1. "Have you learned your lesson?" asked May's teacher.
2. "No, Miss Chapin, and I cannot learn it; it is too hard," replied May.
3. "Have you not been idle, May?" asked the teacher.
4. "I have been idle only a minute," answered May.
5. "Take care of the minutes, May, and your lesson will soon be learned," remarked the teacher.

Who is represented as speaking in each of the foregoing sentences?

Tell the exact words used in each sentence by the speaker.

In which sentences are the exact words of the speaker in the form of a question? In which are they in the form of a statement?

What punctuation mark must always follow a question? What mark must follow a statement?

What other marks beside the commas do you see in the sentences, and where are they?

When a speaker or writer uses the exact words of another in telling what the other has said, the exact words are said to be *quoted*, and they form a **direct quotation**.

A direct quotation is the expression of the thought of another in his own words. It must be inclosed in quotation marks (" "), and, if a complete statement, must begin with a capital.

A comma usually precedes a direct quotation that does not stand at the beginning of a sentence. Punctuation marks that belong to a quotation must stand within the quotation marks.

Titles of books, pictures, poems, or newspapers, also assumed names of writers, etc., are often written with quotation marks; as, "Our Old Home," "The Sistine Madonna," "Gray's Elegy," "The New York Herald," "Oliver Optic" (William T. Adams).

LESSON CXXXII.

INDIRECT QUOTATIONS.

In quoting another person, we are not obliged to use his exact words. We may express his thoughts in our own words. If you will turn to Lesson CXXXI., you will see how easily this may be done.

The sentences marked 1 and 2 might have been written as follows: —

1. May's teacher asked her whether she had learned her lesson.
2. May replied that she had not, and that she could not learn it, because it was too hard.

In the same way, rewrite the sentences marked 3, 4, and 5.

Examine the sentences which have been rewritten, to see whether you can find the exact words of the teacher and of May.

An indirect quotation is the expression of another's thought without using his exact words. Quotation marks are not used in indirect quotations.

LESSON CXXXIII.

QUOTATIONS (*continued*).

Exercise.

(Oral and then Written.)

Change the following to indirect quotations: —

1. My mother said, "Annie, come directly home from school."
2. I replied, "Mother, I will come just as soon as the teacher excuses me."
3. "I feel sure that you will," said mother.

Change the following indirect quotations to direct: —

4. Charlie asked me to lend him my knife.
5. The teacher told us that the birds would soon go south for the winter.
6. Willie asked Charlie how many papers he had sold.
7. Charlie replied that he had sold only twenty-five papers.

LESSON CXXXIV.

QUOTATIONS (*continued*).

A Fable.

A Hare once made fun of a Tortoise. "What a slow way you have!" he said. "How you creep along!"

"Do I?" said the Tortoise. "Try a race with me, and I will beat you."

"You only say that for fun," said the Hare. "But come! I will race with you. Who will mark off the bounds and give the prize?"

"Let us ask the Fox," said the Tortoise.

The Fox was very wise and fair; so he showed them where they were to start, and how far they were to run.

The Tortoise lost no time. She started at once, and jogged straight on. The Hare knew he could come to the end in two or three jumps, so he lay down and took a nap first. By and by he awoke, and then ran fast; but when he came to the end, the Tortoise was already there.

Slow and steady wins the race.

(Oral.)

Are the quotations in this fable direct or indirect? Read the quotations only.

Try to tell the story in your own words, using no direct quotations.

What is a fable? What does this one teach?

Why should the hare and the tortoise be selected to illustrate this fable?

(Written.)

Write the story of *The Hare and the Tortoise* in your own words, and tell what you think it means. Use no direct quotations.

LESSON CXXXV.

VERB FORMS.

The word *break* suggests *breaks, breaking, broke, broken.*
The word *bite* suggests *bites, biting, bit, bitten.*
The word *eat* suggests *eats, eating, ate, eaten.*
The word *drive* suggests *drives, driving, drove, driven.*

The first three words of each set are called **present forms,** the fourth and fifth are **past forms.**

The first three words of each set are used correctly by almost everybody. The last two words of each set cause many errors. The trouble arises from using one for the other.

The *fifth* word in each set is properly used after one of the following words: *have, has, had, having, be, is, am are, was, were, being, been.*

The *fourth* word in each set should never be used after one of these words.

Construct sentences to show that you can use the last two words of the four sets above correctly.

To the Teacher. — Confine the drill to the parts of the verb that cause errors. Review the lesson frequently.

LESSON CXXXVI.

REPRODUCTION.

Read, with your teacher, the following poem, and then write the thoughts in your own words.

Thanksgiving Day.

Over the river and through the wood,
  To grandfather's house we go;
    The horse knows the way
    To carry the sleigh
Through the white and drifted snow.

Over the river and through the wood —
  Oh, how the wind does blow!
    It stings the toes
    And bites the nose,
As over the ground we go.

Over the river and through the wood,
  To have a first-rate play.
    Hear the bells ring,
    Ting-a-ling-ding!"
Hurrah for Thanksgiving Day!

INFORMATION EXERCISE.

Over the river and through the wood,
  Trot fast, my dapple-gray!
    Spring over the ground,
    Like a hunting-hound!
For this is Thanksgiving Day.

Over the river and through the wood,
  And straight through the barnyard gate,
    We seem to go
    Extremely slow, —
It is so hard to wait!

Over the river and through the wood —
  Now grandmother's cap I spy!
    Hurrah for the fun!
    Is the pudding done?
Hurrah for the pumpkin-pie!
                    — L. Maria Child.

LESSON CXXXVII.

INFORMATION EXERCISE.

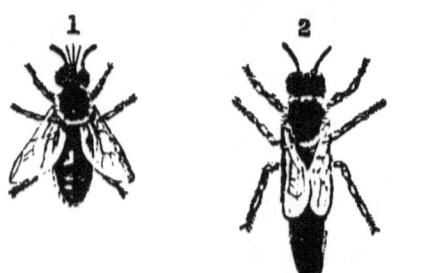

WORKER BEE.   QUEEN BEE.   DRONE.

The Honeybee.

Unlike the spider, the honeybee is a social creature. Great numbers of honeybees live together, and not only work together, but work on a common plan. As so many have to work together, there must be the strictest order and division of labor.

There are three kinds of bees in every hive, — females or queens, males, and workers. The males, which are often called drones, do not work. The workers collect the honey, feed and protect the young, and make the wax with which they build the cells. The males have no stings.

Only one full-grown queen lives in a hive. After she has laid eggs in the cells prepared for them, the workers supply these cells with the pollen of flowers. This is mixed with honey and water, and forms the food of the little white worms that hatch from the eggs. These little worms change into workers, males, or queens.

The worms that become queens are fed with a richer food than is given to the others. Five days after they are hatched they spin cocoons, and in sixteen days more they come out perfect queen bees. The workers and males have a slower growth.

TOPICS FOR STUDY AND CONVERSATION.

Different kinds of bees—queen bees; drones; workers. Hives—honeycomb; wax; cells; eggs; cocoons. Bee-hunting—gathering honey.

LESSON CXXXVIII.

INFORMATION EXERCISE.

THE HONEYBEE (*continued*).

When the little queens are full-grown, the old queen tries to kill them, for she is jealous and wants to reign alone. Either they must be destroyed, or she must leave the hive with a part of the bees, to make another home. But the workers keep watch, and do not let her come near the young queens until they are sure she doesn't mean to leave the hive. In that case, she is allowed to sting and kill all the young females, or queens. If, however, she flies off, followed by many of the bees, a young queen is set free. This queen usually departs with another swarm, as it is called, and the next one will do the same if the hive is still too large.

When a young queen refuses to leave the hive, she fights with the remaining queens, and the one that comes off victorious becomes queen and sole mistress of the hive.

Conversation Exercise.

Is the queen bee a good mother? Which bees may be called protectors? Why? What is meant by "swarming"? What happens when the old queen leaves the hive? Who finally becomes queen of the old hive?

LESSON CXXXIX.

COMPOSITION.

Review very carefully the two preceding lessons, and write what you have learned about the honeybee. First make your notes, and determine the number of paragraphs in your composition.

Any information you have gained from observation or from other books should be used to make your account of the honeybee more complete.

LESSON CXL.

SYNONYMS.

Synonyms are words which have the same or similar meanings; as, *droll, comical; forgive, pardon.*

In the following sentence, the word *own* may be used instead of *possess*, and the meaning will be the same: —

Example: I should like to *possess* a horse and carriage.

The words *possess* and *own* are synonyms.

Find in the third and fourth columns synonyms to the words in the first and second columns.

Examples: gift, present; port, harbor, etc.

port	house	courteous	vacant
gift	brave	harbor	heedless
share	crack	portion	fracture
pursue	careless	present	conceal
empty	fright	follow	alarm
hide	polite	fearless	residence

Construct five sentences which shall contain five of the words in the first two columns, used correctly.

Substitute for the words taken from the first two columns the synonyms taken from the third and fourth.

Which synonyms have exactly the same meaning?

Examples: The teacher made me a *gift* of a beautiful book.
The teacher made me a *present* of a beautiful book.

To THE TEACHER.—The object of this exercise is to teach that while synonyms have *similar* meanings, the meanings are not often exactly the *same.*

LESSON CXLI.

A LETTER.

FRED TO HIS AUNT MARY.

Cold weather — a severe snowstorm — streets blocked — no school. Made a snow man last week — tells how — size — eyes — nose — mouth — arms. Warm weather came on — snow man disappeared.

Write Fred's letter in full.

When and where is your letter dated? What is the "address"? What mark of punctuation follows the "address"? What capital letters are used in the letter because they begin proper names? What capital letters are used because they begin sentences?

What is the conclusion of your letter? What marks of punctuation besides periods have you used?

LESSON CXLII.

STORY FROM PICTURE.

(Oral and then Written.)

SUGGESTIONS.

Describe the picture; that is, tell exactly what you see in it.

Describe the inside of the house as you imagine it, and the family of which you see a part.

Give a history of the family, or a story suggested by the picture.

Every person in the picture must have a name, and also a place in your story.

LESSON CXLIII.

COMPOSITION.

Read the following poem, and then write a composition telling what you think of the lesson it conveys: —

Say No.

Dare to say "No" when you're tempted to drink.
Pause for a moment, my brave boy, and think;
Think of the wrecks upon life's ocean tossed,
For answering "Yes" without counting the cost.

Think of the mother who bore you in pain,
Think of the tears that will soon fall like rain,
Think of the heart and how cruel the blow,
Think of her love, and at once answer "No."

Think of the hopes that are drowned in the bowl,
Think of the danger to body and soul,
Think of sad lives once as pure as the snow;
Look at them now, and at once answer "No."

Think too of manhood with rum-tainted breath,
Think of its end and the terrible death.
Think of the homes that, now shadowed with woe,
Might have been heaven had the answer been "No."

Think of lone graves both unwept and unknown,
Hiding fond hopes that were fair as your own.
Think of proud forms, now forever laid low,
That still might be here had they learned to say "No."

Think of the demon that lurks in the bowl,
Driving to ruin both body and soul.
Think of all this as life's journey you go,
And when you're assailed by the tempter, say "No."

LESSON CXLIV.

PRONUNCIATION EXERCISE.

Pronounce the following words according to the marking: —

kĕpt	sĕv'en	tăs'sĕl
läun'dry	swĕpt	tōw'ard
pär tĭc'ū lar	slĕpt	tī'ny
sŭp pōse'	dánç'ing	tŏss'ĭng
çī'pher	măs'sĭve	brō'ken
de fīne'	de grēe'	em brāçe'

Name the vowel sound in each syllable.

Show clearly the meaning of each word by using it in a sentence.

Review all the exercises in pronunciation that precede this one.

LESSON CXLV.

A LETTER.

AUNT MARY TO FRED.

Was glad to receive a letter from him — surprised to find that he could write so well — thinks he must be a big boy and a good scholar — wants to know about the school he attends, and about his teacher. Tells him of a great snowstorm some years ago — was obliged to walk two miles through the snow — thinks she looked like a snow woman. She is glad that Fred is enjoying the winter.

Write Aunt Mary's letter in full.

LESSON CXLVI.

WORDS OFTEN MISUSED.

Real for very.

Real and *very* have meanings quite unlike. The following sentence shows the correct use of the words: —

> *Example:* Mrs. Ray wears a *real* diamond, and she is *very* proud of it.

Don't for doesn't.

Write, in sentences, the words for which these contractions stand, beginning as follows: —

You do not ——.   Charles does not ——.   I do not ——.
He does ——.   The boys ——.   The boy ——.

Substitute the contractions in your sentences, and you will see their proper use.

Guess for think.

In the following sentences *guess* and *think* are correctly used: —

> *Examples:* I may *guess* what is in your closed hand.
> Blindfolded, I may *guess* who touched me.
> If the clouds look dark, I *think* it will rain.
> It is so cold that I *think* there will be frost to-night.

Complete the following sentences: —

—— what is in my pocket. Shall I be late at school? I —— you will, as it is almost nine. How tall am I? I —— you are four feet ten inches.

Have got for have or has.

Have got means *have obtained*. *Have* when used alone implies *ownership* or *possession*.

We need to use *have got* or *has got* very rarely. We use *have* and *has* frequently.

LESSON CXLVII.

REPRODUCTION.

BARBARA FRIETCHIE.

Read carefully Whittier's poem, *Barbara Frietchie*.

Think of the situation of Frederick among the Maryland mountains, of the season of the year, of the appearance of the great army approaching the town, and of the story of the poem.

Write the story in your own words.

LESSON CXLVIII.

COMBINATION OF STATEMENTS.

Two or more statements may be combined into one sentence, as follows: —

STATEMENTS.

Jessie Brown found a diamond ring.
She was on her way to school.
The ring had been dropped into the mud.

COMBINED.

On her way to school, Jessie Brown found a diamond ring which had been dropped into the mud.

Exercise.

Combine each of the following groups of sentences into one sentence: —

1. Baby Maud has fully recovered her health.
She has been very sick.

2. Our schoolhouse has been rebuilt.
It was burned down.

MEMORY EXERCISE.

3. The birds will return in the spring.
   They go south every autumn.
4. Boston is the largest city in New England.
   It is the capital of Massachusetts.
   It is the metropolis of Massachusetts.
5. President Lincoln was shot by John Wilkes Booth.
   He was in a theater at Washington.
   He died the next day.

Write first two and then three sentences, similar to those above, that may be combined into one sentence.

LESSON CXLIX.

MEMORY EXERCISE.

Study and commit to memory the following poem: —

THE CHILDREN'S HOUR.

Between the dark and the daylight,
   When the night is beginning to lower,
Comes a pause in the day's occupations,
   That is known as the Children's Hour.

I hear in the chamber above me
   The patter of little feet,
The sound of a door that is opened,
   And voices, soft and sweet.

From my study I see in the lamplight,
   Descending the broad hall stair,
Grave Alice, and laughing Allegra,
   And Edith with golden hair.

A whisper, and then a silence:
   Yet I know by their merry eyes
They are plotting and planning together
   To take me by surprise.

A sudden rush from the stairway,
 A sudden raid from the hall!
By three doors left unguarded
 They enter my castle wall!

They climb up into my turret
 O'er the arms and back of my chair;
If I try to escape, they surround me;
 They seem to be everywhere.

They almost devour me with kisses,
 Their arms about me entwine,
Till I think of the Bishop of Bingen
 In his Mouse Tower on the Rhine!

Do you think, O blue-eyed banditti,
 Because you have scaled the wall,
Such an old mustache as I am
 Is not a match for you all?

I have you fast in my fortress,
 And will not let you depart,
But put you down into the dungeon
 In the round-tower of my heart.

And there will I keep you forever,
 Yes, forever and a day,
Till the walls shall crumble to ruin,
 And molder in dust away!
    — HENRY W. LONGFELLOW.

LESSON CL.

REPRODUCTION.

(Oral and then Written.)

Write the story of *The Children's Hour* in your own words.

Tell what you think of Longfellow's home life, and of his love for children. Read his other poems: *Paul Revere's Ride* and *The Village Blacksmith*.

CHAPTER VIII.

LESSON CLI.

CONVERSATION EXERCISE.

COLD COUNTRIES.

Describe the foregoing picture, telling about every kind of object represented.

Find out from your Geography and other books, about the coldest countries — their direction from us, the animals that live there, the houses, food, and occupations of the people.

TO THE TEACHER. — Teachers will find in geography an abundance of material for language lessons. The exercises given in this book are very simple, but they furnish opportunities for pupils to use language intelligently in connection with subjects made familiar through their daily school lessons. Teachers can easily multiply such exercises.

LESSON CLII.

CONVERSATION EXERCISE.

COLD COUNTRIES (*continued*).

Describe the interior of one of the houses, as you imagine it in the evening.

Tell about the seasons in these countries, and about day and night.

What have you read of explorers who have found out about cold countries?

LESSON CLIII.

COMPOSITION.

Arrange topics, and write about cold countries.

LESSON CLIV.

SOUNDS OF LETTERS.

The sounds of the vowels in the words *sir, her, fur*, are exactly alike. They are marked thus: — î, ê, û.

Place a mark over each vowel in these words: *thirsty, burning, prefer, urgent, term, third.*

In the following words, how many different sounds has *th?* — *thee, thin, thus, thick, with, breath, smooth, broth.* In which words is the sound of *th* vocal?

When *th* has a *vocal* sound, it is marked thus: — th. Otherwise it is not marked. In which of the foregoing words should *th* be marked to indicate the pronunciation?

MEMORY EXERCISE.

Exercise.

Indicate the pronunciation of the following words by marking all the letters you can: —

mark	this	rise	rove	cure
give	trap	gem	ask	scene
bulb	stop	roof	curve	foot
move	fruit	wolf	stir	term

LESSON CLV.

PRONUNCIATION.

Pronounce the words below according to the marking: —

ásked	clōtheṣ	crăn' bĕr rў
ăt tăcked'	creek	coûr' te oŭs
a' nў bŏd y (a = ĕ)	drāin	sûr prīṣe'
ca mĕl' o pärd	drȧught (gh = f)	ġē ŏḡ' ra phў

Copy the words, and mark them for pronunciation without the aid of the book. Use each word in a sentence.

LESSON CLVI.

MEMORY EXERCISE.

Read the following poem and commit it to memory: —

THE WONDERFUL WORLD.

Great, wide, wonderful, beautiful world,
With the beautiful water above you curled,
And the wonderful grass upon your breast —
World, you are beautifully dressed!

The wonderful air is over me,
And the wonderful wind is shaking the tree;
It walks on the water and whirls the mills,
And talks to itself on the top of the hills.

You friendly earth, how far do you go,
With wheat fields that nod, and rivers that flow,
And cities and gardens, and oceans and isles,
And people upon you for thousands of miles?

Ah, you are so great and I am so small,
I hardly can think of you, world, at all;
And yet, when I said my prayers to-day,
A whisper within me seemed to say:
"You are more than the earth, though you're such a dot;
You can love and think, and the world cannot."

LESSON CLVII.

INFORMATION EXERCISE.

The Ant.

The ant is a very industrious little insect, and a very skillful workman. There are many different kinds of ants. Some of them make their homes above ground, of grass, wheat stalks, sand, etc., and others burrow in wood or clay, making galleries and chambers.

Among ants there are males, females, and workers, just as among bees. The males and females have wings for a short time. The workers take good care of the eggs, and carry them from one chamber to another, according to the amount of heat desired.

When the little white grubs are hatched, they are as helpless as the bee grubs, and have to be fed and taken care of until old enough to spin cocoons. At the proper time, the workers cut open these cocoons with their jaws and let the little ants out.

Some species of ants have a strange way of going out in great swarms to capture the eggs and cocoons of other tribes of ants. These they carry to their own colonies to hatch, and then make life-long slaves of them.

Topics for Study and Conversation.

The ant, an insect — different kinds — their homes.
Compare the *ants* and the *bees*.
Duties of the workers — care of the grubs.
Cocoons. Slave hunters.

LESSON CLVIII.

COMPOSITION.

Arrange notes for a composition on ants, and then write a full account of them.

LESSON CLIX.

WHO OR WHOM.

Oral Exercise.

Use *who* or *whom* in each of the following questions: -

1. —— is coming into the house with father?
2. To —— did you give the knife?
3. —— do you see on the platform?
4. With —— were you playing?
5. From —— did you receive your new shoes?
6. —— will come with me to the woods?

Ask questions which the following sentences might answer, using *who* or *whom* in each: —

7. I came to school with Mary.
8. Charles bought the apple for the baby.
9. James lent his pencil to his sister.
10. I saw Henry Maple.
11. We did not hear anybody.
12. The baby loves his mother.
13. Susie is standing by her uncle.

Written Exercise.

Write the questions for the foregoing answers.
Write five questions of your own, using the word *whom*, and write the answer after each question.

LESSON CLX.

A LETTER.

Read the letter below, make notes, and write an answer to Cousin May: —

PAXTON, ILL., Oct. 14, 1893.

MY DEAR COUSIN, —

As I sit at my window writing, I am thinking that you, who live so many miles away among the hills of New England, may never have seen one of these vast western prairies.

Can you imagine a whole township of land, yes, many townships, perhaps, as level as the floor in your father's barn, and entirely destitute of trees, and even of shrubs? Well, our prairies in this neighborhood seem perfectly flat, and there is not a tree to be seen except now and then a few which have been planted by the settlers to give shade to cattle or to serve as a wind-break. Even stones are seldom found, and one may travel many a mile without seeing even a pebble in the black soil of our dusty roads.

I have been told that these prairies were once under water, — that they were the beds of great seas; but I am not wise enough really to know whether these sayings are true or not. I do know, however, that you would like to see these great plains, which must look so much like the vast ocean of which you speak. Some of the western prairies are called rolling prairies, because they look like the sea when it is in motion. I have seen such prairies myself, many miles away, in another state.

Sometime I will tell you about the wheat, corn, rye, and oats that grow here; but I forget — you must have learned about these things in your Geography.

Well, dear cousin, if I have told you nothing but what you knew before, at least I have kept my promise to write you a long letter. Now, please write me all about your home, which must be very different from mine.

Your loving cousin,

MAY.

THE COMMA.

LESSON CLXI.

THE COMMA.

You have already been required to use the comma in the heading, salutation, and close of letters. Please write a heading, a salutation, and a conclusion, and punctuate them correctly.

Notice the use of the comma in the following sentences: —

1. Mother, I cannot tell you what has become of the horse.
2. I cannot tell you what has become of the horse, mother.
3. I cannot tell you, mother, what has become of the horse.

You will see that the word *mother*, which denotes address, is *set off* by one or two commas in each sentence.

1. James, Charles, and Henry gathered apples, pears, and grapes.
2. A kitten likes to run, jump, and play.

In these sentences, the comma is used to separate words forming a **series**. Point out the series in the first sentence; in the second.

Exercise.

Copy the following sentences, using the comma where required: —

1. Where were you Nellie?
2. Corn wheat oats and rye are called grain.
3. Jamestown Va. June 16 1888.
4. I tried to find you Miss Johnson but I could not.
5. We read write sing and recite at school.
6. Yours sincerely James Graham.
7. John was Washington Irving an American?
8. Poetry refines purifies and elevates the mind.
9. What has become of your top James?

LESSON CLXII.

REPRODUCTION.

(Oral and then Written.)

Read the *Wreck of the Hesperus*, by H. W. Longfellow, and try to understand it.

Write the story without using direct quotations.

LESSON CLXIII.

VERB FORMS.

(Oral and then Written.)

Name four other words suggested by each of the following: *go, give, draw, fly, forget, blow, break, choose, thrive, shake.*

go	goes	going	went	gone
give	——	——	——	——
draw	——	——	——	——
fly	——	——	——	——
forget	——	——	——	——
blow	——	——	——	——
break	——	——	——	——
choose	——	——	——	——
thrive	——	——	——	——
shake	——	——	——	——

You will probably write and use the first three words of each set correctly, provided you know how to spell them.

Recollect that *have, has, had, be, is, was, are, were, being, been*, should never be used before the *fourth word*.

Use the fourth and fifth words of each set in sentences.

LESSON CLXIV.

MEMORY EXERCISE.

Read and commit to memory the following poem: —

LITTLE BROWN HANDS.

They drive home the cows from the pasture,
 Up through the long shady lane,
Where the quail whistles loud in the wheat fields,
 That are yellow with ripening grain.
They find, in the thick waving grasses,
 Where the scarlet-lipped strawberry grows.
They gather the earliest snowdrops,
 And the first crimson buds of the rose.

They toss the new hay in the meadow;
 They gather the elder-bloom white;
They find where the dusky grapes purple
 In the soft tinted October light.
They know where the apples hang ripest,
 And are sweeter than Italy's wines;
They know where the fruit hangs the thickest
 On the long, thorny blackberry vines.

They gather the delicate seaweeds,
 And build tiny castles of sand;
They pick up the beautiful seashells, —
 Fairy barks that have drifted to land.
They wave from the tall, rocking tree-tops
 Where the oriole's hammock-nest swings;
And at night time are folded in slumber
 By a song that a fond mother sings.

Those who toil bravely are strongest;
 The humble and poor become great;
And so from these brown-handed children
 Shall grow mighty rulers of state.
The pen of the author and statesman, —
 The noble and wise of the land, —
The sword, and the chisel, and palette
 Shall be held in the little brown hand.

LESSON CLXV.

INFORMATION EXERCISE.

The Beaver.

The beaver is found in North America and in the Old World. In the winter, five or six of these animals live together as a family, in a house built in the water, of sticks, mud, and stones. These houses are round on top, and the entrance is under water.

The beaver spends a great part of its life in the water, and is always found near the banks of some stream or lake. His hind paws are webbed, like those of a duck or swan, so that they form paddles with which the animal pushes itself along when in the water.

If the stream is too shallow, so that the entrance to the house might be closed in the winter by the ice, the beavers living near first build a dam at some suitable place in the stream. For this purpose, in the latter part of summer, they cut down trees with their sharp teeth, and float the trunks down the stream to the place selected for the dam. These are then sunk to the bottom by means of stones. More trees are then added, until the dam is high enough to answer the purpose of the beavers. These trees, with branches and stones, are afterward firmly plastered together with mud.

The houses are then built in the deep water above the dam. The walls of these houses, or lodges, as they are usually called, are very thick; and as, in winter, the mud of which they are chiefly composed is frozen into a solid mass, the beavers have a safe refuge from all their enemies.

COMPOSITION.

Read the foregoing account of the beaver, and carefully study the picture. From these two sources you will learn something of the habits of this curious animal. Try to find from other sources something about his size, food, industry, manner of life, and his use to man. Find out, if you can, how and in what parts of this country he is trapped. Then prepare notes and write an orderly account of him.

LESSON CLXVI.

REVIEW.

(Oral and then Written.)

Note carefully how each of the following nouns is printed: *horse's, child's, men's, wife's, colts', calves', babies', birds', monkey's, mouse's, kittens', robin's.*

Tell whether the nouns are singular or plural.

Tell how each noun should be written in the other number.

Use each noun in a written sentence.

Rewrite each sentence, changing the number of the noun which you are required to use.

LESSON CLXVII.

SYNONYMS.

Each word in the first two columns has a synonym in the third or the fourth column.

get	brave	assist	gladden
aid	wish	procure	want
please	see	gladness	behold
mirth	great	merry	large
gay	aged	bold	old
tell	error	narrate	mistake
task	build	work	erect

Arrange the synonyms in pairs and use each word in a sentence.

Exercise.

For the word in Italics in each of the following sentences, substitute its synonym; and tell whether it may properly be used.

1. With money one can *get* power, but not love.
2. A boy may do much to *aid* his mother.
3. It will *please* your teacher if you say "Good morning."
4. The monkey caused great *mirth* in school.
5. A *gay* company of girls just went by.
6. The captain likes to *tell* his adventures to the children.
7. A *brave* boy will always tell the truth.
8. The prisoner made a *bold* attempt to escape, and the officer was obliged to *procure* assistance.
9. I *wish* to go out with you.
10. Longfellow was a *great* poet.
11. This *aged* man is hale and hearty.

To the Teacher. — This exercise is designed to show that synonyms, though similar in meaning, are not always interchangeable.

LESSON CLXVIII.

COMBINATION OF STATEMENTS.

Combine the following sentences, as in Lesson CXLVIII.

1. Frank Day has a beautiful pony.
   The pony was given to Frank last Christmas.
2. Our school had a pleasant time at the picnic.
   The picnic was near a small lake.
   The picnic was held in a grove.
   The grove was of pine trees.
3. Benjamin Harrison was President of the United States.
   Mr. Harrison's home is in Indianapolis, Ind.
4. A noble dog saw a child in the water.
   The dog sprang into the water.
   The dog brought the child safely to shore.
5. London is the largest city in the world.
   London is the capital of England.
   London is situated on the Thames River.
6. George Washington was the first President of the United States.
   George Washington is often called "The Father of his Country."
7. Chicago is situated on Lake Michigan.
   Chicago is the largest city in Illinois.
   Chicago is the greatest grain market in the world.
8. A large part of Illinois consists of prairie land.
   Much of this prairie land is very level.
   The prairie land is fertile.
9. The eastern shores of Massachusetts are washed by Massachusetts Bay.
   Massachusetts is often called "The Old Bay State."

Write two sentences and combine them into one.
Write three sentences and combine them into one.

LESSON CLXIX.

MEMORY EXERCISE.

Read and commit to memory the following poem: —

Nobody's Child.

Only a newsboy, under the light
 Of the lamp-post plying his trade in vain;
Men are too busy to stop to-night,
 Hurrying home through the sleet and rain.

Never since dark a paper sold;
 Where shall he sleep, or how be fed?
He thinks as he shivers there in the cold,
 While happy children are safe abed.

Is it strange if he turns about
 With angry words, then comes to blows,
When his little neighbor, just sold out,
 Tossing his pennies, past him goes?

"Stop!" — some one looks at him, sweet and mild,
 And the voice that speaks is a tender one.
"You should not strike such a little child,
 And you should not use such words, my son!"

Is it his anger or his fears
 That have hushed his voice and stopped his arm?
"Don't tremble," these are the words he hears;
 "Do you think that I would do you harm?"

"It isn't that," and the hand drops down;
 "I wouldn't care for kicks and blows;
But nobody ever called me son,
 Because I'm nobody's child, I s'pose."

O men! as ye careless pass along,
 Remember the love that has cared for you;
And blush for the awful shame and wrong
 Of a world where such a thing could be true!

— Phœbe Cary.

CHAPTER IX.

LESSON CLXX.

CONVERSATION EXERCISE.

WARM COUNTRIES.

Examine very carefully the picture at the head of this chapter, describe it, and tell what it suggests to you.

Learn, from your Geographies and from other books, all you can about warm countries — their direction from us, the kind of people and the animals that live there, how the people live and dress, their houses, food, and occupations.

Contrast the seasons, the day and night, and the vegetation of very cold countries, with those of very warm countries.

Imagine a journey and its difficulties, in the hottest part of South America, and tell about your travels.

Read books of travel giving accounts of life and adventures in Africa or in southern Asia. Such books may be found in almost any public or private library in the neighborhood.

LESSON CLXXI.

COMPOSITION.

Write all that you have learned in Lesson CLXX. about warm countries, following the order of the topics below. Divide your composition into four paragraphs.

1. Wet season; dry season; vegetation.
2. People who live in Central America; in Africa; in India; their food and clothing; houses; business.
3. A journey through some hot country; mode of travel; disagreeable experiences; camping out.
4. Contrast some hot country with your own, showing why it is pleasanter to live here than there.

LESSON CLXXII.

LETTER WRITING.

In preceding lessons you have written letters from *notes* or *suggestions* given in the book. Of course, before you can become a good letter writer, you must be able to write without the help of suggestions made by others.

In this chapter you will be required to depend almost entirely upon yourself; but, after a little practice, you will find that you can write letters as good as those on which you received help.

Below are the notes made by a boy who visited his grandfather in Rutland, Vt., in July, 1894. From these notes he wrote a letter to his mother.

NOTES.

Arrival. Description of journey. Account of farm, cattle, horses, etc. Account of fishing-trip one cloudy day. How I helped grandfather about the farm. A little homesick; shall return next week.

Suppose it to be vacation, and that you are visiting relatives either in the city or country.

Arrange notes for a letter to your father.

LESSON CLXXIII.

LETTER WRITING (*continued*).

Prepare notes from which letters could be written on the following subjects: —

1. A visit to the North in winter.
2. An account of a picnic.
3. A boating excursion, including an accident.

LESSON CLXXIV.

WORDS OFTEN MISPRONOUNCED.

Note carefully the marking of each of the following words, and then pronounce each very distinctly: —

äl' mond (*l* is silent).	äunt	mū ṣē' ŭm
räsp' ber ry (*p* is silent).	brōoch	be nēath'
Är' ab	jŭst	hĭs' to rў
Är' a bĭc	jäunt	hụr räh'

LESSON CLXXV.

REPRODUCTION.

(Oral and then Written.)

Read the poem, *The Leak in the Dike*, by Phœbe Cary.

Learn about dikes, and why they are needed. Why are they needed in Holland?

From a second reading, make notes from which to write. Write the story.

LESSON CLXXVI.

DERIVATIVE WORDS.

You will notice that the word *form* appears in each of the following words: —

reform	forming	reformer
inform	formless	information
uniform	formation	deformity

The word *form* is called the **root** of all of the other words because it is the most important part; or it may be said that the other words are derived from the root word. Hence they are called derivative words, or **derivatives.**

Each of the derivative words in the first column is formed by prefixing a syllable to the root word. The syllables thus used are called **prefixes.**

The derivative words in the second column are made by placing syllables after the root word. Syllables so used are called **affixes** or **suffixes.**

How are the derivatives in the third column formed?

Use in a sentence each of the words derived from *form*.

To THE TEACHER. — Do not require children in this grade to give the meaning of the different prefixes and suffixes.

INFORMATION EXERCISE. 143

LESSON CLXXVII.

INFORMATION EXERCISE.

Cotton.

Cotton seed was planted as an experiment by some of the earliest settlers of the Southern States; but the plant was little known, except as a garden ornament, until after the Revolution.

About a hundred years ago the first sea-island cotton was raised on the coast of Georgia. The seeds were obtained from the Bahamas, having been introduced there from another group.

The seed of the cotton is planted in March or April. The plants grow rapidly, and reach a height of from three to five feet. Later on, when the pale-yellow flowers drop off, a triangular pod is left. This ripens during the latter part of summer, and, bursting open, shows the white cotton, in which are hidden black or green seeds according to the variety. Cotton seed yields an oil which is sometimes used in place of olive oil.

Topics for Study and Conversation.

When and where was cotton first raised in this country? Finest variety — where from — why so called. Planting seeds — blossom — pod, or boll. Cotton seeds — cotton gins — Eli Whitney. Uses of cotton — cotton clothing — cotton factories.

LESSON CLXXVIII.

COMPOSITION.

Write about cotton, following the order of the Topics.

LESSON CLXXIX.

DIVIDED QUOTATIONS.

Sometimes the words of a speaker or writer come between the parts of a quotation which he is making.

Example: " 'Twas yours," he said, "but now 'tis mine."

Dictation Exercise.

A humming-bird met a butterfly, and, being pleased with the beauty of his person and the glory of his wings, made an offer of perpetual friendship.

"I cannot think of it," was the reply, "as you once spurned me, and called me a drawling dolt."

"Impossible!" exclaimed the humming-bird, "I have always had the highest respect for such beautiful creatures as you."

"Perhaps you have now," said the other, "but when you insulted me I was a caterpillar. So, let me give you a piece of advice. Never insult the humble, as they may some day become your superiors."

VERB FORMS.

LESSON CLXXX.

QUOTATIONS (*continued*).

(Oral and then Written.)

Tell the meaning of the following words, selected from Lesson CLXXIX., and use each in a sentence: —

person	dolt	drawling	exclaimed	advice
glory	reply	perpetual	respect	humble
offer	spurned	impossible	insulted	superiors

Change the direct quotations in the Dictation Exercise to indirect quotations.

Rewrite the entire dictation exercise, expressing the same thoughts without using any of the words whose meaning you have given, and using only indirect quotations.

What *synonyms* have you used for any words in this exercise?

LESSON CLXXXI.

VERB FORMS.

Write four derivative words from each of the following root words: — *shake, freeze, fall, see, write, grow.*

Examples: Shake, shakes, shaking, shook, shaken.
Freeze, freezes, freezing, froze, frozen.

After completing the five sets of words, notice how the second and third words in each set are made from the first.

Use in a sentence the fourth word in each set.

After what words is the fifth word generally used?

Use in a sentence the last word in each set.

Review Lesson CXXXV., in Chapter Six.

LESSON CLXXXII.

A LETTER.

Robert Austin lives in Providence, R.I., where he is attending the Oxford Grammar School. His cousin, George Eliot, lives in a country town in New Jersey. Robert is getting tired of school work, and is looking forward to vacation, when he hopes his cousin will visit him. So he writes to George, invites him to come, and suggests some of his plans for the vacation.

Make notes from which Robert's letter could be written.

Write Robert's letter in full.

To the Teacher.— From the notes made by the class, select such as seem most suggestive, and write them on the blackboard. It may seem best to require all the pupils, at first, to write from the same notes.

LESSON CLXXXIII.

WORDS OFTEN MISUSED.

Like for As.

As is correctly used in the following sentences: —

Examples: Try to write *as* I do.
James is tall and straight, *as* his father was.

Few worse errors in English can be made than to use *like* instead of *as* in such sentences as the foregoing.

Exercise I.

Complete each of the following sentences with *like* or *as:* —

My brother looks —— me.
I wish I could talk —— you do.

SPELLING EXERCISE.

Make two sentences, in each of which *like* shall be used correctly.

Make two sentences, in each of which *as* shall be used correctly.

Funny for odd or strange.

The root of *funny* is *fun.* So, whatever is *funny* should tend to make us laugh.

Exercise 2.

Fill the blanks with the proper words.

Uncle John told very —— stories to make us laugh.
A camel is a —— looking animal.
The man had a —— gait.

Most for almost.

Exercise 3.

Supply the proper words in the following sentences: —

—— boys like apples.
We are —— there.
—— all of us prefer to speak correctly.
He said that he was —— well again.

LESSON CLXXXIV.

SPELLING EXERCISE.

The following exercises will show you how to study a spelling lesson. You should prepare the lessons on your slate, or with paper and pencil.

gut ter	at tic	car riage	gim let
may or	pitch er	cof fee	vel vet
sa loon	bu reau	sir up	cam bric
gar ret	scis sors	vin e gar	cal i co

Arrange the words alphabetically. Classify them as to syllables, and mark the accents. Use each word in a thoughtful sentence.

LESSON CLXXXV.

SPELLING EXERCISE.

Prepare the following exercise as in Lesson CLXXXIV.

an gel	stom ach	writ ten	birth day
sail or	fin ger	in di rect	doubt ful
schol ar	trou sers	re al ly	swin dle
mo ment	stock ing	mild ly	cin na mon
tor pe do	shoul der	cush ion	im ag ine

(Oral.)

Which words are accented on the first syllable? Which on the last syllable? Which words are derivatives, and from what words are they derived? Use each word in a sentence.

LESSON CLXXXVI.

SYNONYMS.

In the second column of words below, a synonym may be found for each word in the first column:—

allow	costly
imitate	injury
feast	deceive
detect	devour
consume	discover
border	conduct
construct	banquet
behavior	build
expensive	edge
damage	mimic
cheat	permit

WORDS TO USE AFTER *IS* AND *WAS*. 149

Write each word with its synonym.
Use each word in the first list in a thoughtful sentence. In which of your sentences may the synonyms be substituted without changing the meaning?

Example: consume and devour are synonyms.

A bear will *consume* a great deal of meat.
A bear will *devour* a great deal of meat.
A boy will sometimes *consume* much time in doing little work, but he will not *devour* the time.

LESSON CLXXXVII.

WORDS TO USE AFTER *IS* AND *WAS*.

The following sentences are correct: —

1. Was it *he* who spoke to *me?*
2. It was *I* who spoke to *him*.
3. Is it *she* who is talking to *us?*
4. It is *we* who are talking to *her*.
5. It is *they* who are to blame, and I blame *them*.

Exercise.

Complete the following sentences with one of these words: *I, me, he, him, she, her, we, us, they, them:* —

1. Who is there? It is ——.
2. Is it —— that you wish to see?
3. I know it was —— because I saw ——.
4. Do you think it was ——? No, it was ——.
5. It is —— who were speaking to ——.
6. Who is there? It is only ——. You need not be afraid of ——.
7. That is my mother. I know it is ——. I hear —— calling.
8. Father, was that you? Yes, Charlie, it was ——. Come to ——.
9. Who sang "Home, Sweet Home"? It was —— and —— who sang it.

LESSON CLXXXVIII.

COMBINATION OF SENTENCES.

Exercise.

Combine the sentences in each set into one sentence: —

1. Maine is the largest of the New England States.
Maine is noted for its lumber.

2. Portland is the largest city in Maine.
Portland was the birthplace of Longfellow.
Longfellow was a famous American poet.

3. Washington served his country in the Revolution.
Washington served his country as President.
Washington retired to Mount Vernon.
Mount Vernon is on the Potomac River.

4. John Adams was the second President of the United States.
John Adams was the father of John Quincy Adams.
John Quincy Adams was the sixth President of the United States.

LESSON CLXXXIX.

MEMORY EXERCISE.

Read and commit to memory the following poem: —

NOBILITY.

True worth is in *being*, not *seeming*, —
 In doing, each day that goes by,
Some little good, — not in the dreaming
 Of great things to do by and by.
For whatever men say in blindness,
 And spite of the fancies of youth,
There's nothing so kingly as kindness,
 And nothing so royal as truth.

MEMORY EXERCISE.

We get back our mete as we measure,
   We cannot do wrong and feel right,
Nor can we give pain and gain pleasure,
   For justice avenges each slight.
The air for the wing of the sparrow,
   The bush for the robin and wren,
But alway the path that is narrow
   And straight, for the children of men.

We cannot make bargains for blisses,
   Nor catch them like fishes in nets;
And sometimes the thing our life misses
   Helps more than the thing which it gets.
For good lieth not in pursuing,
   Nor gaining of great nor of small;
But just in the doing, and doing
   As we would be done by, is all.

Through envy, through malice, through hating,
   Against the world, early and late,
No jot of our courage abating —
   Our part is to work and to wait.
And slight is the sting of his trouble
   Whose winnings are less than his worth;
For he who is honest is noble,
   Whatever his fortunes or birth.
                — ALICE CARY.

Read the following poems selected from Alice Cary's writings: *Old Maxims, Telling Fortunes, The Wise Fairy, Story of a Blackbird, Waiting for Something to Turn Up, Recipe for an Appetite, In the Dark.*

CHAPTER X.

LESSON CXC.

DESCRIPTION.

You have already had considerable practice in writing compositions, and have learned something about the use of capital letters and punctuation marks. Some of your compositions have been called **stories**, some **letters**, and some **reproductions**.

Sometimes you will be called upon to describe what you have seen; and in order to do this well, you must notice very carefully everything that will be likely to interest those who read your description.

The following base-ball notes may help you in the preparation of the next lesson. Study them carefully, and notice that they are so arranged as to suggest the number of paragraphs in the composition.

NOTES.

A bright, sunshiny day. Saturday — no school.

Our town boasts a famous "nine." The club that played with them to-day. How we went to the grounds. Rather hot and dusty. Incident.

Play begins. Our boys have bad luck. How the crowd screamed and whistled! Luck changes. Our boys ahead by one run. Umpire unfair. Game a tie.

Tenth inning decides it. Our boys beaten. The ride home. Better luck next time.

LESSON CXCI.

NOTES FOR COMPOSITION.

Make notes for a composition on each subject below: —
1. A fishing excursion.
2. My visit to a menagerie.
3. My first attempt at skating.
4. My first ride on a bicycle.

Composition.

From the four sets of notes, select one set, and write a full account of the subject.

LESSON CXCII.

DERIVATIVES.

Oral Exercise.

governor	misgovern	writer	rewriting
governing	ungovernable	rewrite	unwritten
government	misgovernment	written	rewritten
governess	governorship	writings	writable

Name the root word for each group of words.
In each word, name the prefix or suffix, or both.
Give the meaning of each word as nearly as you can.

Written Exercise.

Rewrite the words in each column, separating the root word from the prefixes and suffixes.

Write sentences which will show that you know the meaning of the root words, and of all the words derived from them.

154 SUGGESTED STORIES.

LESSON CXCIII.

SUGGESTED STORIES.

[Select only one for a lesson.]

1. Write a story suggested by this picture of two children in a boat. The boat is floating down the harbor towards the sea.

2. Think of a picture of a young lad sitting at the window of a residence near a schoolhouse. He is wrapped in a shawl, and looks pale and sickly. A vase of flowers stands upon a small table near the window. What story can you tell about this lad?

3. A boot is overheard telling its life story to an old cat lying on a rug before the fire. The boot has had a hard time of it, as it has been worn by a careless boy who loved play better than work. Tell the story that was poured into the old cat's ear.

A LETTER.

4. A piece of chalk lay on the teacher's table, in plain sight of the class, and for a whole day saw all that was going on. At night, after the pupils were dismissed, the chalk had a long talk with its neighbor, and told some strange things about the school in general and the behavior of the pupils in particular.

Write the story that the chalk told, and see if your classmates will enjoy it as well as the chalk's neighbor did.

Under the direction of your teacher write your story on the blackboard, and correct all the faults as your classmates point them out.

Copy the corrected story on paper, and give it to your teacher.

To THE TEACHER. — Only one or two compositions per day can be thus copied upon the blackboard and corrected.

LESSON CXCIV.

A LETTER.

Suppose one of your classmates to be ill. He (or she) has been absent from school several weeks. Write such a letter to the absent pupil as you would like to receive under similar circumstances. Speak of your teacher and of the work of the class. Relate some interesting happenings that would probably interest and amuse your friend.

Under the direction of your teacher, copy your letter upon the blackboard, and then correct the errors as they are pointed out by your classmates.

Rewrite the letter upon paper, and hand it, free from errors, to your teacher.

LESSON CXCV.

THE REPLY.

Write an answer to the letter in the preceding lesson. Tell of some of the pleasures of the sickroom — how very kind your mother and sisters have been; how brother Tom has even given up his play to read aloud to you from an interesting book.

Speak of the doctor, and of the many friends who have called since you have been able to receive company. Show by your letter that even sick people may be cheerful and good-natured.

LESSON CXCVI.

QUOTATIONS.

It is usual to make complete paragraphs of long quotations from books or letters.

Double marks are generally used for a quotation; but single marks (' ') are used when one quotation occurs within another.

When direct quotations are complete statements, they should begin with **capital letters**; but if the quotation is an incomplete statement, the capital is frequently omitted.

Dictation Exercise.

1. It has been well said, "The tongue is a little member and boasteth great things."
2. "The question now is," said he, "how shall we know what are good books?"
3. "Be ready to come when I call you," said his mother.
4. "The greatest of faults," says Carlyle, "is to be conscious of none."

INFORMATION LESSON. 157

5. "On one occasion," says Whittier, "I was told that a foreigner had applied to my mother for lodging. 'What if a son of mine were in a strange land?' she said to herself."

Notice that the quotations are separated from the rest of the sentence by punctuation marks.

LESSON CXCVII.

INFORMATION LESSON.

Frogs.

Frogs lay their eggs in the water. Before the egg is many days old, it is hatched, and out comes an odd little thing with a large head, a long flat tail, and a wedge-shaped body. This is called a tadpole.

For a few days it has a tuft of soft pink threads on each side of its head. These are the gills, which enable the tadpole to breathe in the water. It lives the life of a fish, and finds all its food in the water. But soon a wonderful change takes place; its gills disappear, and lungs form in the chest. After this it can no longer breathe in the water, but must rise to the surface for air.

Four legs gradually grow out, and at the same time the tail disappears. The animal is now a perfect frog, and spends its time partly on land and partly in the water. In winter it crawls into a hole and sleeps there until spring.

A frog may produce a thousand eggs in a year, but very few eggs produce young ones that live to reach winter retreats.

TOPICS FOR STUDY AND CONVERSATION.

1. Eggs — where they are laid, color, size.
2. Tadpoles — description, gills, head, body, tail.
3. Describe the changes that take place.
4. Tell how the frog swims — how it catches its food.
5. Describe his winter quarters.

TO THE TEACHER. — Lessons in Natural History are of little value if unaccompanied by observation.

LESSON CXCVIII.

NEIGHBORHOOD STUDY.

TOPICS FOR CONVERSATION.

1. Places one mile distant from your schoolhouse; two miles; five miles; ten miles.
2. Public conveyances — stages, horse cars, steam cars.
3. Parts of the neighborhood that are level, hilly, mountainous.
4. Water in the vicinity — brooks, rivers, ponds, lakes, and other waters with which they are connected.

COMPOSITION.

Write what you have learned by the preceding study, dividing your composition into four paragraphs.

LESSON CXCIX.

VERB FORMS.

The boy or girl who will give the following words close thought can learn their correct use in a few days.

sit	sits	sitting	sat	sat
set	sets	setting	set	set
lie	lies	lying	lay	lain
lay	lays	laying	laid	laid

Exercise.

Complete the following sentences with words chosen from the table above: —

1. I —— the pointer on the table. It is —— there now.
2. —— the chair on the floor, and —— down in it. I am —— in it, and have —— here an hour.
3. Mary —— in bed this morning until eight o'clock. If she had —— there much longer she would have missed her breakfast.
4. Where does the snow —— on the ground all the year?
5. I have —— still five minutes; I cannot —— still any longer.
6. The dog is —— near the fire.
7. The baby —— her head on the dog, and there she —— now fast asleep.

LESSON CC.

REPRODUCTION.

Read Holmes's *Ballad of the Boston Tea Party*. Learn all you can about the "Old South" meetinghouse, and the famous meeting held there just before the "party." Also learn what you can about the "Indians," who they really were, and what they did.

For a second lesson, make notes, and write an account of the incident and the poem.

LESSON CCI.

WORDS OFTEN MISUSED.

Will for shall.

In asking questions, *will* should not be used before *I* or *we*.

Exercise I.

Complete the following sentences with the proper word: —

1. Where —— we go when school is out?
2. —— I bring the book to you?
3. When the work is done, what —— I do?
4. —— we ever learn to use *shall* correctly?

Can for may.

May should be used either in asking or granting permission. We *can* do what we have strength or ability to do.

Exercise 2.

Supply the proper word in the following sentences: —

1. Mrs. Gray, —— I take your pencil for a moment? Certainly you ——.
2. I should like to go home now; —— I?
3. I —— solve that problem; —— you?
4. He —— go home, but you —— not.
5. I —— jump across the brook. —— I do so, Alice?

Construct three questions, showing the correct use of *shall*.

Construct three questions, showing the correct use of *may*.

LESSON CCII.

MEMORY EXERCISE.

Read and commit to memory the following poem: —

ABOU BEN ADHEM.

Abou Ben Adhem (may his tribe increase)
Awoke one night from a deep dream of peace
And saw, within the moonlight in his room,
Making it rich and like a lily in bloom,
An angel writing in a book of gold:
Exceeding peace had made Ben Adhem bold,
And to the Presence in the room he said,
"What writest thou?" The vision raised its head,
And with a look made of all sweet accord,
Answer'd, "The names of those who love the Lord."
"And is mine one?" said Abou. "Nay, not so,"
Replied the Angel. Abou spoke more low,
But cheerily still; and said, "I pray thee then,
Write me as one that loves his fellow-men."

The angel wrote and vanished. The next night
It came again with a great wakening light,
And show'd the names whom love of God had bless'd,
And lo! Ben Adhem's name led all the rest.
— *Leigh Hunt.*

STUDY AND CONVERSATION.

1. Tell what the poet means by the following expressions: *may his tribe increase; dream of peace; the presence; sweet accord; a great wakening light; whom love of God had blessed; Ben Adhem's name led all the rest.*
2. What do you think the poem means?
3. Tell the story in your own words.

LESSON CCIII.

WHO AND WHICH.

Who is used in speaking of persons. *Which* is used in speaking of lower animals and things.

Exercise 1.

Insert *who* or *which*, and such other words as may be necessary, after each Italicized word.

MODEL.

The *tree* is one hundred years old.
The *tree which stands on the corner* is one hundred years old.

1. It was General *Grant*.
2. My *friend* is now in New York.
3. This *lesson* is very difficult.
4. I cut down the *tree*.
5. The dog caught the *rabbit*.
6. The *dog* caught the *rabbit*.

Exercise 2.

Complete the following sentences : —

1. My older brother whom ——.   Do you know who ——?
2. I saw the man to whom ——.   It was he who ——.

LESSON CCIV.

WORDS OFTEN MISUSED.

Expect for *suspect, suppose,* or *presume.*

Whenever *expect* is correctly used it refers to future time.

Exercise 1.

Complete the following sentences with one of the words at the head of the lesson : —

1. James's mother —— him to return at four P.M. to-morrow.
2. I —— that he has returned already, as I saw a valise in the hall.

3. You have not watered the plants for a week; I —— that they are all dead.
4. Was Charles late at school this morning? Oh! I —— so, he is almost always late.
5. I —— that Alice has finished the painting.
6. I —— him to tell me the truth, but I strongly —— that he has not done so.

Use the words correctly in sentences of your own.

Plenty for plentiful.

The following sentences will show you the correct use of the two words : —

We have had plenty *of rain this summer.*
The rain this summer has been plentiful.

Exercise 2.

Complete the following sentences either with *plenty* or with *plentiful:* —

1. Have you —— of money?
2. No, money is never —— with me.
3. Strawberries are cheap when they are ——
4. How —— the apples are this autumn!
5. There is a —— supply of wheat there, and also —— of corn.

Stop for stay, and stopping for staying.

To *stop* is to cease from motion.
To *stay* is to *remain.*

Exercise 3.

Complete the following sentences with *stop, stay.* etc. : —

1. The train will —— at the station, and will —— there two hours.
2. George has been —— at his uncle's nearly all winter.
3. Do not —— on your way east, as you will wish to —— with me a long time in Boston.
4. If you do not —— that noise, I shall not —— here with you.

LESSON CCV.

NEIGHBORHOOD STUDY.

Topics for Conversation.

1. Vegetables, including trees — kinds and uses.
2. Wild flowers — names and description.
3. Business of the people — farming, different kinds of manufactures, trade or commerce.
4. Beautiful scenery — describe it; tell in what its beauty consists.
5. Public buildings or other works of art, such as monuments, statues, etc.

To the Teacher. — It may be necessary to divide such lessons as this into two or three parts, in order to give the pupils more time to investigate the different subjects.

LESSON CCVI.

COMPOSITION.

Write upon one or more of the topics given in the preceding lesson, giving a full and interesting account of what you have learned and how you learned it.

LESSON CCVII.

DERIVATIVES.

First, tell from what root word each word below is derived, and then use the root word in a sentence.

broken	gone	frozen	blown
done	given	fallen	shaken
bitten	drawn	seen	spoken
eaten	flown	written	stolen
driven	forgotten	grown	taken

WORDS OFTEN MISUSED. 165

Notice that the words all end in *n* or the sound of *n*. Use the word *have* with every one. Name the five forms of which each word in the list is one. (See Lesson CLXXXI.)

LESSON CCVIII.
HISTORICAL LETTER.

Read the story of the battle of Lexington. Form in your mind a picture of the route from Boston to Lexington which was followed by the British. Picture the farmhouses on the route; the country people leaving their work to watch the soldiers; the men and older boys taking their guns and following through the woods and fields; the scene on Lexington Common; the destruction of the stores in Concord; the retreat to Boston; the Americans hiding behind walls, trees, and houses, and firing upon the British soldiers. Also read Bryant's stirring poem, *Seventy-Six*, Holmes's *Lexington*, and Longfellow's *Paul Revere's Ride*. Then prepare notes for a letter.

Suppose you were living near Lexington on the 19th of April, 1775, and saw all that has been described to you in the story of the battle of Lexington. Write a letter to your cousin living in England, and give an account of what you saw and heard on that memorable day

LESSON CCIX.
WORDS OFTEN MISUSED.
Some for somewhat.

The following sentences indicate the correct use of *some* and *somewhat* : —

Some *of the boys are very noisy to-day.*
My father *is* somewhat *better this morning.*

Exercise 1.

Complete the following sentences by inserting *some* or *somewhat*: —

    You came to church —— late last Sunday.
    Is that boy tired? No, but he is —— lazy.

Quantity for number.

We should use *number* in speaking of things that may be counted; as, a *number* of sheep, a *number* of cattle. We say, a *quantity* of oats, a *quantity* of hay.

Exercise 2.

Use the word *number* in three different sentences.
Use *quantity* in three different sentences.

Only.

The difficulty in using *only* arises from not knowing where to place it in a sentence.

Exercise 3.

Notice and explain the different meanings conveyed by the word *only* in the following sentences: —

    1. *Only* the boy snatched the apple.
    2. The boy *only* snatched the apple.
    3. The boy snatched *only* the apple.

Exercise 4.

In the following sentences use *only* in as many different places as possible, and explain the changes in meaning: —

    1. My sister read the Bible this morning.
    2. Little George hit his brother in the eye.
    3. Boys and girls whisper in school.

LESSON CCX.

ADVERTISEMENTS.

1. Write an advertisement for a situation as book-keeper in some large store. State your qualifications and give references.
2. Write such an answer to your advertisement as you would like to receive.
3. Advertise the loss of a watch, giving some particulars, and offering a reward.
4. Write an advertisement, stating that you have found a watch which the owner can have by proving property and paying charges.

LESSON CCXI.

DICTATION.

Exercise.

After writing the following proverbs from dictation, tell their meaning in your own words: —

1. The sleep of the laboring man is sweet.
2. The borrower is servant to the lender.
3. Faithful are the wounds of a friend.
4. The wicked flee when no man pursueth.
5. Give me neither poverty nor riches.
6. Remember now thy Creator in the days of thy youth.
7. Think much, write little, speak less.
8. Wisdom is the principal thing, therefore get wisdom.
9. Be not righteous overmuch.
10. Cast thy bread upon the waters, for thou shalt find it after many days.
11. A word fitly spoken is like apples of gold in pictures of silver.

12. Look not thou upon the wine when it is red, . . . at the last it biteth like a serpent, and stingeth like an adder.
13. A wise son maketh a glad father.
14. A soft answer turneth away wrath.

LESSON CCXII.

LETTERS AND NOTES.

1. Write a letter of recommendation for a personal friend.
2. Write an application for a position as teacher in a neighboring town.
3. Write a note of thanks for some favor received.
4. Write to a friend, extending an invitation to dine with you.

LESSON CCXIII.

HISTORICAL LETTER.

Read from some good history the story of the landing of the Pilgrims, and read Bryant's poem, *The Twenty-Second of December*. Learn all you can of the *Mayflower*, and some of the most noted persons who came in that vessel; also read about their sufferings during the first winter. Finally, read *The Courtship of Miles Standish*.

Afterwards make notes of what you have learned about the Pilgrims.

Suppose yourself to have been one of the Pilgrims, and that you were one of the soldiers who fought under the leadership of Miles Standish.

Write a letter to some friend in England, giving an account of your experiences.

LESSON CCXIV.

INFORMATION EXERCISE.

Salt.

1. You have how many kinds of salt before you? Examine them carefully. Do they look alike? How do they differ in appearance? Touch each kind to your tongue. Do they taste alike?

2. What uses are made of salt at your home? Which kind is most commonly used? For what is the other kind used? Why is it sometimes used on an icy sidewalk?

3. Mention some articles of food which would not taste well without salt.

To the Teacher. — Each pupil should be supplied with some common salt, and also with a small piece of rock salt. For information, let the pupil consult the best encyclopedia at hand.

Study.

Find out what you can about the manufacture of common salt. Also, read all you can find about salt springs and salt mines.

LESSON CCXV.

COMPOSITION.

Write what you have learned about the different kinds of salt. Tell what salt is used for, how it is obtained, and where it is most abundantly found.

Use the hints given in the preceding lesson, and divide your composition into paragraphs.

LESSON CCXVI.

INFORMATION EXERCISE.

Wool..

The thick, soft growth on the skin of a sheep is called wool. This wool, if left to itself, would drop off in summer, for the sheep has then no need of it to keep him warm. But instead of allowing it to drop off, men cut it off just in time to save it. The wool sheared or

cut from a sheep is called a *fleece*. The fleeces are cleaned and then sent to a factory, where the wool is spun into thread, and then woven into cloth.

Wool is obtained from other animals, such as the alpaca, cashmere goat, etc., but the sheep furnishes the greater part of that which is used in making clothing.

TOPICS FOR STUDY AND CONVERSATION.

Wool, what kind of product?
Sheep, different kinds — some of the most valuable.
Sheep-shearing — explain the process.

Parts of our country where the most wool is produced.
Other countries where wool is plentiful.
How it is brought to this country.
Woolen manufactures. Worsteds.
Uses of wool and of woolen cloths.
Describe what you see in the picture.
In what parts of the year is most wool used for clothing?

Composition.

Write from the topics all that you have learned about *wool*.

LESSON CCXVII.

Memory Exercise.

Read and commit to memory the following poem: —

To a Waterfowl.

    Whither, 'midst falling dew,
While glow the heavens with the last steps of day,
Far, through their rosy depths, dost thou pursue
    Thy solitary way?

    Vainly the fowler's eye
Might mark thy distant flight to do thee wrong,
As, darkly painted on the crimson sky,
    Thy figure floats along.

    Seek'st thou the plashy brink
Of weedy lake, or marge of river wide,
Or where the rocking billows rise and sink
    On the chafed ocean side?

    There is a Power whose care
Teaches thy way along that pathless coast,
The desert and illimitable air, —
    Lone wandering, but not lost.

All day thy wings have fanned,
At that far height, the cold, thin atmosphere,
Yet stoop not, weary, to the welcome land,
Though the dark night is near.

And soon that toil shall end;
Soon shalt thou find a summer home, and rest
And scream among thy fellows; reeds shall bend
Soon o'er thy sheltered nest.

Thou'rt gone, the abyss of heaven
Hath swallow'd up thy form; yet on my heart
Deeply hath sunk the lesson thou hast given,
And shall not soon depart.

He who, from zone to zone,
Guides through the boundless sky thy certain flight,
In the long way that I must tread alone,
Will lead my steps aright.
—*W. C. Bryant.*

Study and Conversation.

1. What part of the day is referred to in the first stanza? What reasons can you give for your answer? What is the author's thought in the last two lines of this stanza?

2. Show the connection of thought between the first and second stanza.

3. In the third stanza, ask and answer three questions suggested by the poet.

4. Give in your own words the meaning of the fourth stanza.

5. What does the poet mean by *the cold, thin atmosphere,* in the fifth stanza?

6. Explain the meaning of the next three stanzas. What lesson is referred to in the last but one?

VERB FORMS.   173

LESSON CCXVIII.

CONVERSATION EXERCISE.

OUR OWN COUNTRY.

You have studied about cold countries, and also about warm countries. Now contrast our houses, our clothing, and our food, with the houses, clothing, and food of people living in cold countries, and also with those of people living in warm countries.

Contrast our modes of traveling and our manufactures with those of cold and of warm countries.

Give an account of any other advantages which you think we have over the people of those countries, and tell why you would rather live in our own country.

Tell some of the advantages which the inhabitants of cold countries enjoy. Of warm countries.

COMPOSITION.

Write about *Our Own Country*, and use as notes the hints found in the conversation exercise in Lesson CCXVIII.

LESSON CCXIX.

VERB FORMS.

1. From each of the following root words form a derivative by adding *s* or *es:* — *bring, begin, blow, come, catch.*

2. Form a derivative from each by adding *ing.*

3. From each word form a derivative which may be used after *have, has,* or *had.*

4. What derivative from each word might be used in telling an event that took place last week?

5. What are prefixes and suffixes? Give examples.

CHAPTER XI.

LESSON CCXX.

THOUGHTS, IDEAS, SENTENCES, WORDS.

John caught a rabbit in his trap.

The preceding group of words expresses a **thought**. The thought can neither be seen nor heard. We speak and write **words**. We think thoughts, and express them by words. A word alone does not express a thought, but it suggests an **idea**. Thoughts are made of connected, or related, ideas. **Sentences** are made of words.

Exercise.

How many sentences are there in the exercise below? Why are they sentences? How many thoughts are expressed?

How many words are in the first sentence? the second? the third? the fourth?

Point out the words in each sentence that do not suggest any idea to you.

    1. The poor man worked hard for his family.
    2. The squirrel builds his nest in a tree.
    3. Four new books lie on my table.
    4. The steamer *Priscilla* runs to New York.

What does a sentence express? Can you see the sentences above? Can you see the thoughts? Are there any sentences that you cannot see? What do you call them? Are the sentences that you can only hear, spoken or written sentences? Of what are such sentences made? Of what are spoken words made?

LESSON CCXXI.

THE SENTENCE.

A group of words expressing a complete thought is a sentence.

Exercise I.

Which of the following groups of words are sentences, and which are not? Tell why.

1. The rain is falling quietly.
2. Are you studying?
3. The road is very
4. Lo! the poor Indian.
5. Winter has its pleasures.
6. Every question has

Exercise 2.

Which of the sentences below make statements? Which ask questions? Which express commands or make entreaties?

1. There is a tide in the affairs of men.
2. Do the leaves fall before the fruit ripens?
3. Give us, this day, our daily bread.
4. How many times must you be told?
5. The race is not always to the swift.

Sentences that make statements are called **declarative** sentences; those that ask questions are **interrogative** sentences; those that express commands or make entreaties are **imperative** sentences.

Declarative and imperative sentences should be followed by periods (.); an interrogative sentence should be followed by an interrogation mark (?).

Sentences sometimes express emotion or strong feeling; as, *How dear to my heart are the scenes of my childhood!*

Such sentences are called **exclamative**, and should be followed by an exclamation point (!).

LESSON CCXXII.

SUBJECT AND PREDICATE.

Exercise I.

Make complete sentences of the following: —

1. The robin redbreast ——.
2. Two swans, all white as snow, ——.
3. The wind ——.
4. The faint old man ——.
5. The apple trees ——.
6. —— began the bloody battle.
7. —— grew darker as the sun went down.
8. —— is never at rest.
9. —— is called a tyrant.
10. —— are driven away.

In each of the first five sentences above you have supplied the words that make an assertion. This part of a sentence is called the **predicate**.

In the last five sentences you have supplied the words that tell of what the assertion is made. This part of a sentence is called the **subject**.

The part of a sentence which represents and sometimes describes the thing of which something is asserted is the subject.

The part of a sentence which makes an assertion is the predicate.

INVERTED SENTENCES. 177

LESSON CCXXIII.

ANALYSIS.

Exercise.

My thoughts | are my companions.

In the exercise below, separate each subject from its predicate by a vertical line.

Give the reason why one part of each sentence is the subject and the other the predicate.

1. The full ripe corn bends in waves of golden light.
2. Autumn fires burn fiercely in the forest.
3. I saw old Autumn in the misty morn.
4. Obedience is a part of religion.
5. Almost everybody becomes a reader in our age.

The word which names the person or thing of which an assertion is made is called the **simple subject**.

Point out the simple subject in each sentence.

LESSON CCXXIV.

INVERTED SENTENCES.

When the subject of a sentence stands before the predicate, the sentence is said to be in its **natural order**.

When the whole or a part of the predicate stands before the subject, the sentence is **inverted**.

Example: Day by day the dead leaves fall and melt.
The dead leaves fall and melt day by day.

Exercise.

Rewrite each of the following sentences, placing the subject before the predicate.

Draw a vertical line between the subject and predicate. Point out the simple predicate in each sentence.

1. All green and fair the summer lies.
2. Deep in the forest arbutus doth hide.
3. Night by night the blast wails in the trees.
4. Again has come the springtime.
5. To-day the spring is in the air and in the blood.
6. To one tall-towered mill a long street climbs.
7. Slow and sure comes up the golden year.
8. Unto the pure all things are pure.

LESSON CCXXV.

EXERCISE ON SENTENCES.

From the following lines, select as many good sentences as you can.

Tell whether the sentences you have selected are declarative, interrogative, or imperative.

Point out the subject of each declarative sentence, and tell why you think it is the subject.

Point out the predicate of each declarative sentence, and tell why you think it is the predicate.

What matter how the night behaved?
What matter how the north-wind raved?
Blow high, blow low, not all the snow
Could quench our hearth-fire's ruddy glow.

We tread the paths their feet have worn,
  We sit beneath their orchard trees,
  We hear, like them, the hum of bees
And rustle of the bladed corn.

Clasp, Angel of the backward look,
The brazen covers of thy book.
. . . .
Shut down and clasp the heavy lids.

COMPELLATIVES.

LESSON CCXXVI.
ANALYSIS OF INTERROGATIVE SENTENCES.

In an interrogative sentence, the arrangement of the subject and predicate is usually **inverted**.

DECLARATIVE. *Each exercise | must be well written.*
INTERROGATIVE. *Must | each exercise | be well written?*

In the declarative form, the subject generally stands first and the predicate second.

In the interrogative form, a part of the predicate usually stands first, the subject second, and the rest of the predicate third.

Before analyzing an interrogative sentence, therefore, it is well to change it to the declarative form.

Exercise.

Change the following sentences to the declarative form, and then separate the subject from the predicate : —

1. Can gray hairs make folly venerable?
2. Have I not had to wrestle with my lot?
3. Is it in heaven a crime to love too well?
4. Hast thou a charm to stay the morning star?
5. What news do you bring us from the king?
6. Did you not know his name?

LESSON CCXXVII.
COMPELLATIVES.

In the sentence, *Annie, will you go to the post office for me?* for what purpose is the word *Annie* used?

Under what circumstances could you make the request without using Annie's name?

IMPERATIVE SENTENCES.

Is the sentence interrogative or imperative?
What is the subject of the sentence? the predicate?

As the name, *Annie*, is used to call, or compel, the attention of the person addressed, it may be called a **compellative.** As you have seen, it forms no part of the subject or predicate, but is entirely independent of the sentence.

The compellative should be separated from the rest of the sentence by a comma or commas.

Exercise.

In each of the following sentences name the compellative.

Point out the subject and the predicate.

1. Gentlemen, have you agreed upon a verdict?
2. Thou, O Lord, shalt endure forever.
3. Mr. President, I have but a few words to say.
4. Now, friend William, I will grant your request.
5. Venerable men, you have come down to us from a former generation.
6. Cassius, I am armed in honesty.
7. O, Liberty! my spirit felt thee there.
8. Yes, social friend, I love thee well.
9. Will you follow me, my brother?

LESSON CCXXVIII.

IMPERATIVE SENTENCES.

Imperative sentences are used in giving commands and in making entreaties. As such commands and entreaties are usually made to some one who is present, the name, or word standing for the name, of the one addressed is often omitted. If an imperative sentence contains a compella-

USES OF WORDS IN SENTENCES. 181

tive, the latter must not be confounded with the subject. The subject is usually either *thou* or *you*.

Stand (thou) *fast, lone sentinel of God,*
On proud Athena's noblest hill.

In this sentence, *thou* (understood) is the subject, and *lone sentinel of God* is a compellative.

Exercise.

Analyze the following imperative sentences, and tell why each sentence is imperative.

Name the subject and the predicate. Point out the compellative if there is one.

1. Let not Ambition mock their useful toil.
2. Drink deep, or taste not the Pierian spring.
3. O gallant captain, show some pity
   To a lady in distress.
4. Break, O Sea, on thy cold gray stones.
5. Sail on, O Union, strong and great.

LESSON CCXXIX.

USES OF WORDS IN SENTENCES.

Every word in a sentence has some use, and may be classified according to its use.

The holly branch shone on the old oak wall.

In this sentence the word *holly* tells the kind of branch; *branch* tells what shone; *shone* tells what the branch did; *on the old oak wall* tells where the holly shone; *wall* tells on what it shone; *old* and *oak* tell the kind of wall.

To THE TEACHER. — For the present, omit the *articles* in such exercises.

Exercise.

Tell the use of each word in the following sentences: —

1. There mountains rise, and circling oceans flow.
2. Simple men admire studies, and wise men use them.
3. The gleaming rushes lean a thousand ways.
4. He hears the parson pray and preach.
5. Never spend your money before you earn it.
6. The price of wisdom is above rubies.

LESSON CCXXX.

NOUNS.

The word *noun* means *name*.

New York is a large city.

In this sentence, *New York* is a noun because it is a name. The word *city* is also a noun because it is a name.

A word, or a group of words, used as a name, is called a noun.

Exercise.

Point out the nouns in the following sentences, and tell why they are nouns: —

1. Rip Van Winkle entered the house.
2. Dame Van Winkle had always kept it in good order.
3. The lonely chambers rang for a moment with his voice.
4. A large wooden building stood in its place.

A noun that denotes but one object is said to be in the **singular number**; as, *man, boy, horse, tree, mouse.*

A noun that denotes two or more objects is said to be in the **plural number**; as, *men, boys, horses, trees, mice.*

LESSON CCXXXI.

PROPER NOUNS AND COMMON NOUNS.

If we speak of *Mary*, or *George Washington*, we mean some particular person. But when we use the word *man* or *paper*, we use a word that may apply to any one of a great number of persons or of things of the same sort.

Names that refer to some particular person, place, or thing are called **proper nouns**; as, *Mary, George Washington, St. Stephen's Church*.

Names that refer to classes of persons or things are called **common nouns**; as, *man, boy, ocean, teacher, paper, ink, pen, island*.

Exercise 1.

PROPER NOUNS.	COMMON NOUNS.
George, Henry, Simon	boy, man
Atlantic, Pacific, Indian	ocean

Place at the right of each group of words below, an appropriate class name, as in the examples above: —

PROPER NOUNS.

Sarah, Susan, Grace
Connecticut, Amazon, Hudson
Carlo, Bruno, Fido
Columbia, Harvard, Yale

Exercise 2.

Place at the right of each common name some appropriate proper name: —

COMMON NOUNS.

teacher	island	boy	city	ocean
warrior	friend	nation	river	bay

A proper noun must always begin with a capital letter. A common noun does not begin with a capital letter unless it is the first word in a sentence, or is used in a title.

LESSON CCXXXII.

POSSESSION, OR OWNERSHIP.

Nouns in the singular number are made to denote possession, or ownership, by the addition of an apostrophe and *s* (*'s*); as, *Mary's hat, the boy's sled, the horse's ear.*

Nouns in the plural number that do not end in *s* are made to express ownership in the same way; as, *men's boots, children's dresses, the oxen's yoke.*

But if the plural noun ends in *s*, the apostrophe only is added; as, *boys' hats, cows' horns, mules' ears.*

Exercise 1.

Use the following nouns in sentences so that they will express ownership: —

horse	cow	mule	boy	kitten
bird	girl	cat	calf	woman
man	ox	lady	grocer	gentleman

Exercise 2.

Use in sentences the plural number of the same nouns, and use them so that they will denote ownership.

LESSON CCXXXIII.

PRONOUNS.

There are a few words that we often use instead of nouns. Thus in speaking of ourselves we use the words *I, my, me, we, our, us.* In speaking to a person, we say *you, your,* and sometimes *thou, ye, thy,* or *thee.* In speaking of persons or things we say *he, she, it, his, her, its, they, their, them.*

These little words so often used are called **pronouns**, because *pro-noun* means *for a noun.*

A word used instead of a noun is called a pronoun.

It might sometimes be very awkward for us to use a person's name in speaking of him or to him, and more awkward still if we always had to call our names in speaking of ourselves. In speaking about *James*, we might be obliged to say: —

James came to visit our school last week, and while here, James sat near the teacher. The teacher asked James where James had been at school before, etc.

The name for which a pronoun stands is called its **antecedent.** The antecedent of a pronoun is not always expressed.

Rewrite the sentence just given about James, and use a pronoun instead of his name whenever it will sound better to do so.

Exercise.

In the following sentences, point out the pronouns, and tell which refer to one person or thing, and which to more than one. Which refer to a person who is speaking? Which to a person spoken to? Which to a person or thing spoken of?

1. I am writing.
2. Did you speak to him?
3. She is very young.
4. We played together.
5. He ran to get it.
6. I sold my watch.
7. The book belongs to me.
8. Did you buy them?
9. The girls tore their gowns.
10. Her lesson is very hard.

LESSON CCXXXIV.

PRONOUNS (*continued*).

Like nouns, pronouns are in the **singular** number when they refer to but one person or thing. Those that denote more than one person or thing are in the **plural** number.

Nouns and pronouns that denote the *speaker* are said to be in the *first person*. Those that denote the person *spoken to* are in the *second person*. Those that denote the person or thing *spoken of* are in the *third person*.

Pronouns that show by their form (spelling) whether they are in the first, second, or third person, are called **personal pronouns**.

LIST OF PERSONAL PRONOUNS (*for Reference*).

	SINGULAR.	PLURAL.
The speaker. First Person.	I, my, mine, me.	We, our, ours, us.
The person spoken to. Second Person.	Thou, thy, thine, thee.	Ye, you, your, yours.
The person or thing spoken of. Third Person.	He, his, him; she, her, hers; it, its.	They, their, theirs, them.

Exercise.

Name each pronoun in this exercise, and point out its antecedent.

Point out the pronouns that have no antecedents expressed.

1. A wise man will make haste to forgive, because he knows the true value of time, and will not suffer it to pass away in unnecessary pain.

2. That he was the author of the work we believe to have been the opinion of all his friends.

3. Where is the true man's fatherland?
Is it where he by chance is born?

4. To him who in the love of nature holds
Communion with her visible forms, she speaks
A various language.

LESSON CCXXXV.

COMPOUND PERSONAL PRONOUNS.

The syllable *self* (plural *selves*) is often added to a personal pronoun, thus forming what is called a **compound personal pronoun**; as, *myself, themselves.*

Exercise 1.

Select from the list of personal pronouns on page 186 those that will take the syllable *self.*

Select from the same list those that will take the syllable *selves.*

Exercise 2.

From the following sentences, select the pronouns, and tell why they are pronouns.

Point out the antecedents of the pronouns.

What pronouns have no antecedents expressed?

What pronouns are compound?

1. Who would be free, himself must strike the blow.
2. Our remedies oft in ourselves do lie.
3. Why don't you speak for yourself, John?
4. He himself has said it.
5. Help yourself and others will help you.
6. Who gives himself with his alms feeds three;
Himself, his hungering neighbor, and me.

LESSON CCXXXVI.

ADJECTIVES.

It is sometimes necessary to point out or describe more fully the object which is named by a noun. For instance, instead of saying, *Boys are picking cherries*, I may wish to tell the number of boys, and so I say, *Two boys are picking cherries*. In describing a field, I may say, *The beautiful, green field bordered the river bank.*

Words used to point out more fully, or describe, the objects designated by nouns and pronouns, are called adjectives.

Exercise.

Those tall green trees in the pasture belong to old Mr. Brown.

In this sentence, *those* points out the trees as distant, *tall* indicates their height, and *green* their color; while *old* shows us which Mr. Brown is meant.

Point out the adjectives in the sentences below, and tell for what purpose each is used.

1. The moon that once was round and full
   Is now a silver boat.

2. And she was fair and very fair,
   Her beauty made me glad.

3. The old man keeps in remembrance the happy days of his childhood.

4. Tell us not, sir, that we are weak, unable to cope with so formidable an adversary.

5. The promises of Hope are sweeter than roses in the bud.

6. Sweet are the uses of adversity,
   Which, like the toad, ugly and venomous,
   Wears yet a precious jewel in his head.

ADJECTIVES.

LESSON CCXXXVII.

ADJECTIVES (*continued*).

Adjectives expressing number, as, *one, two, first, second*, etc., are called **numeral** adjectives.

Two men were in the wagon.

In this sentence, the word *two* is a numeral adjective describing the noun *men*, by telling how many men there were.

Adjectives made from proper names are called **proper** adjectives.

Mrs. Lincoln has just returned from a European trip.

In this sentence, *European* is an adjective describing the noun *trip*. It is a proper adjective because it is made from the proper noun *Europe*.

A **proper** adjective must always begin with a capital letter.

Exercise.

In the following sentences, select all the adjectives, and tell why they are adjectives. Tell how each adjective describes the noun to which it refers.

Which are numeral adjectives, and which are proper adjectives? Tell why.

1. An English gentleman had two sons. The elder son, who was eager for adventure and weary of home, obtained his father's permission to go abroad. Ten years later, a traveler, ragged and dusty, stopped at an inn near the father's estate. He asked the landlord about the father of the two sons. "Oh, he's dead!" said the landlord; "been dead these five years; poor old man! dead and forgotten long ago!"

2. Anon from the belfry
Softly the Angelus sounded, and over the roofs of the village
Columns of pale blue smoke, like clouds of incense ascending,
Rose from a hundred hearths, the homes of peace and contentment.
Thus dwelt together in love these simple Acadian farmers.

LESSON CCXXXVIII.

VERBS.

In the sentence, *Mary studies*, what word tells what Mary does?

Is that word the whole or only a part of the predicate?

In the sentence, *Mary studies her lesson*, what word tells what Mary does? Is that word the whole or only a part of the predicate? For what purpose are the rest of the words in the predicate used?

The word used in a sentence to make an assertion is called a verb.

Exercise I.

Separate the subject from the predicate in each of the following sentences.

Point out the word in each sentence that makes an assertion.

1. Fishes swim.
2. Birds fly.
3. I study.
4. James ran a race.
5. The waves dash against the rocks.
6. The dogs worry the sheep.
7. The lights twinkle from the rocks.
8. A statesman placed himself at the head of his countrymen.
9. Italy bought the Bonaparte papers.
10. The sun shines on the evil and on the good.
11. Ten thousand fleets sweep over thee in vain.
12. God created the heavens and the earth.
13. Cowards die many times before their deaths;
    The valiant never taste of death but once.

VERB PHRASES.

LESSON CCXXXIX.

VERB PHRASES.

In the preceding exercises, you were able to point out one word in each sentence that made an assertion. This word was called a verb.

In many sentences, however, two or more words are required to make an assertion.

The boy will go as soon as possible.

In this sentence, the two words, *will go*, make the assertion.

The boy has been gone a week.

In this sentence, three words, *has been gone*, are required to make the assertion.

These groups of words which are often required to make assertions are called **verb phrases.**

Exercise.

Separate each subject from its predicate by a vertical line or lines.

Point out the verbs and also the verb phrases

1. The fishermen spread their nets in the sun.
2. I can hardly see the stars.
3. The condor of the Andes flies very high.
4. Can the stars be seen on cloudy nights?
5. The storm grows more furious every minute.
6. The girl has not given a word of explanation.
7. Our forefathers purchased liberty with their blood.
8. The poet lived in a quaint old house by the river.
9.   How doth the little busy bee
        Improve each shining hour.

LESSON CCXL.

ADVERBS.

Now the tiny birds build their nest, and securely fasten it to the twigs with bits of thread which they gather here and there for that purpose.

In this sentence, *now* tells when the birds build their nest; *securely* tells how they fasten it to the twigs; and *here* and *there* tell where they gather the threads.

Exercise 1.

Tell what the words in Italics in the following sentences are used for, or tell what questions they will answer:—

1. Evil-doers are *generally* punished.
2. Speak *gently* to the erring.
3. All exercises should be written with *very* great care.
4. He that *never* felt a wound jests at scars.
5. After life's fitful fever he sleeps *well*.

Exercise 2.

First read each sentence in Exercise 1, omitting the word in Italics. Next, read each sentence without omitting the word in Italics. Then tell which word in the sentence is modified (strengthened or weakened) by the word in Italics.

The words in Italics are called **adverbs** because they are often added to verbs to modify them. Very frequently, however, they modify adjectives or other adverbs.

Examples: He is a *very* good boy. (Adverb modifying an adjective.)
She speaks *too* rapidly. (Adverb modifying an adverb.)

An adverb is a word used to modify the meaning of a verb, an adjective, or another adverb.

PHRASES. 193

LESSON CCXLI.

PHRASES.

The trees in the garden are tall and straight.

The group of words *in the garden*, in the sentence above, is needed to modify, or describe, the meaning of the noun *trees* by telling what trees are meant.

As the word *trees* is a noun, the group of words which modifies it must be an adjective. (See page 188.)

To distinguish this *modifier* from the *simple adjective*, we call it an **adjective phrase.**

A similar group of words used as an adverb would be called an **adverb phrase**; as, *He is walking in the garden.* Here, *in the garden* tells where he is walking, and is, therefore, an adverb.

A group of words, used as a part of speech, and having neither subject nor predicate, is a phrase.

Exercise.

Point out the phrases below, and tell whether they are adjective or adverb, and why: —

1. Great clouds of smoke rose from the chimneys.
2. The river in the valley is full of water.
3. The sail in the harbor was very pleasant.
4. The captain of the boat sailed through the dangerous passage with great skill.
5. The steamer struck an iceberg near the coast of Newfoundland.
6. Flocks of sea gulls fly fearlessly about the ship, or float gracefully upon the water.
7. Earth is here so kind that just tickle her with a hoe and she laughs with a harvest.
8. The best thing I know between France and England is the sea.
9. He was so good that he would pour rose water on a toad.

13

194 CONJUNCTIONS.

LESSON CCXLII.

PREPOSITIONS.

Exercise I.

In the sentences below point out the phrases, and tell whether they are adjective or adverb.

* 1. The leaves of the book are uncut.
2. In 1066 A.D. the battle of Hastings was fought.
3. The picture on the wall was painted by a celebrated artist.
4. Heaven from all creatures hides the book of fate.

The last word in each phrase above is a noun or a pronoun. The first word in all such phrases (*of*, *in*, *on*, *to*, *by*, etc.) is called a **preposition** (placed before).

A word used before a noun or a pronoun to show its relation to another word in the sentence is called a preposition.

The noun or pronoun used with a preposition in making a phrase is called its **object**.

A preposition connects the noun or pronoun which follows it with the word modified by the phrase.

Point out the prepositions in the sentences above, and tell what they connect.

LESSON CCXLIII.

CONJUNCTIONS.

Horatio was busy. Henry was busy.
Horatio and Henry were busy.

Here the two predicates of the first two sentences are alike, and the two statements are combined by omitting one of the predicates and connecting the two subjects by *and*.

SENTENCES, SIMPLE AND COMPOUND. 195

Horatio fished. Horatio caught nothing.
Horatio fished, but caught nothing.

These two sentences are combined by omitting one subject (as the subjects are alike) and using the word *but* to connect the two predicates.

Exercise I.

Combine the following statements, as above. Tell what words are connected, and how: —

1. Mary works steadily. Mary works well.
2. Michael Angelo was a painter. Michael Angelo was a sculptor.
3. Lottie can sing. Lottie can play.

A word used to connect words, phrases, or sentences is called a conjunction.

Exercise 2.

Point out the conjunctions in the sentences below, and tell what they connect: —

1. A large elm stands between the house and the river.
2. Brazil is regarded as a land of mighty rivers and virgin forests.
3. Life is short but art is long.
4. Some ran for the woods, and others plunged into the river.

LESSON CCXLIV.

SENTENCES, SIMPLE AND COMPOUND.

A simple statement, question, or command may be a complete sentence; as, *William is an honest boy.* Or it may form only part of a sentence; as, *William is an honest boy, but he does not like books.*

A sentence that contains but one statement, question, or command is called a **simple sentence**.

A sentence that contains two or more independent statements, questions, or commands, joined together by one or more conjunctions, either expressed or understood, is called a **compound sentence**.

Exercise.

Which of the following sentences are simple ? Analyze them.

Separate the compound sentences into independent simple sentences, and analyze them.

1. Some men are born great, some achieve greatness, and some have greatness thrust upon them.
2. A man without hope is of no good use to the world.
3. Seek, and ye shall find.
4. A change came o'er the spirit of my dream.
5. Night's candles are burnt out, and jocund day
Stands tiptoe on the misty mountain tops.

LESSON CCXLV.

INTERJECTIONS.

Words like *oh, O, ah, pshaw, humph, hurrah, alas*, etc., expressing sudden emotion on the part of the speaker or writer, do not form any part of the sentence; that is, they belong neither to the subject nor to the predicate. They are called **interjections** (thrown in, or thrown between).

A word used to express strong feeling, and not connected with any other word in the sentence, is called an interjection.

Exercise.

Tell what feelings are expressed by the interjections in each sentence below: —

1. Pshaw ! I do not believe the story.
2. Ah! what have you been doing?
3. Aha! I have found you out!
4. He came, alas ! but it was too late.
5. Hurrah, hurrah! a single field hath turned the chance of war.

INDEX.

Abbreviations, 19, 20, 102, 103.
Abou Ben Adhem (Hunt), 161.
Accented Syllables, 52.
Addresses, 92.
Adjective phrase, 193.
Adjectives, 188, 189, 192.
Adverb phrase, 193.
Adverbs, 192.
Advertisements, 167.
Æsop (Extract), 26, 44.
Affixes, 142.
Afternoon Nap, The (Reproduction Exercise), 104.
Alcott, Louisa M. (Extract), 29.
Almost, most, 147.
Analysis, 177.
Animals, 33, 44.
Ant, The (Information Exercise), 128.
Antecedent, 185.
Apostrophe, 74, 75, 88, 89, 184.
Are, is, 15, 16, 21, 80, 83.
As, like, 146.

Ballad of the Boston Tea Party (Holmes), 159.
Barbara Frietchie (Whittier), 122.
Beaver, The (Information Exercise), 134.
Bell of Atri, The (Longfellow), 76.
Bird's Story, A (Reproduction Exercise), 22.
Björnson Björnstjerne (Extract), 37.
Blacksmith, The (Information Exercise), 105.
Boys Wanted, 76.
Breve, 28.
Brown Thrush, The (Larcom), 63.
Bryant, William C. (Extract), 171.

Can, may, 160.
Capitals, 6, 7, 8, 19, 42, 45, 46, 60, 108, 110, 156, 184, 189.
Cary, Alice (Extract), 150.
Cary, Phœbe (Extract), 138.
Caterpillar, The (Information Exercise), 78.
Chapter One, 5; Two, 24; Three, 45; Four, 61; Five, 78; Six, 92; Seven, 109; Eight, 125; Nine, 134; Ten, 152; Eleven, 174.
Chapters, 86.
Cherry Buds, Clapp (Information Exercise), 35.
Child, L. Maria (Extract), 113.
Children's Hour, The (Longfellow), 123.
Clapp, H. L. (Extracts), 35, 78.

Classification, 40, 58.
Cold Countries (Conversation Exercise), 125.
Combined Statements, 122, 123, 137, 150.
Comma, 110, 131, 180.
Command, 195.
Common Names, or Nouns, 61, 183.
Compellatives, 179, 180, 181.
Complimentary Close, 96.
Composition Writing, 10, 23, 37, 42, 56, 60, 62, 65, 72, 74, 79, 85, 88, 91, 116, 119, 126, 129, 135, 140, 144, 152, 153, 158, 164, 169, 170, 173.
Compound Personal Pronouns, 187.
Conclusion of Letter, 92, 96.
Conjunctions, 194, 195.
Consonants, 68, 69.
Contractions, 88.
Conversation Exercises, 38, 39, 44, 51, 56, 116, 125, 139, 173.
Cotton (Information Exercise), 143.
Coverings of Animals (Conversation Exercise), 44.
Craik, Mrs. (Extract), 41.

Dandelion (Memory Exercise), 49.
Dates, 20, 46.
Days, 19, 60, 89.
Declarative Sentences, 175, 179.
Derivative Words, 142, 153, 164, 173.
Description, 152.
Dictation Exercises, 7, 15, 19, 20, 31, 45, 46, 58, 78, 89, 136, 167.
Direct Quotations, 109, 110, 156.
Dissyllables, 31.
Divided Quotations, 144.
Doesn't, don't, 121.

Envelopes, 99.
Exclamation Point, 176.
Exclamative Sentences, 176.
Expect, suspect, suppose, presume, 162.

First Snow Fall, The (Lowell), 107.
Force of Habit, The (Mann), 106.
Form of Letter, 92.
Four Bulls and the Lion, The (Æsop), 44.
Frogs (Information Exercise), 157.
Funny, odd, strange, 147.

Games, 18.
Goose and the Golden Eggs, The (Reproduction Exercise), 82.
Grandpapa (Mrs. Craik), 41.

198 INDEX.

Guess (Memory Exercise), 66.
Guess, think, 121.
Hare and the Tortoise, The (Reproduction Exercise), 111.
Hare got, have, has, 121.
He, him, 80, 149.
Heading of Letter, 92, 93, 94.
Her, she, 80, 149.
Him, he, 80, 149.
Historical Letter, 165, 168.
Honeybee, The (Information Exercise), 114.
Hunt, Leigh (Extract), 161.
Hyphen, 30.

I, me, 80, 149.
Ideas, 174.
Imperative Sentences, 175, 180, 181.
Indirect Quotations, 110, 111.
Information Exercises, 35, 50, 64, 73, 78, 87, 105, 114, 115, 128, 134, 143, 157, 169, 170.
Initials, 9.
Insects (Information Exercise), 73.
Interjections, 196.
Interrogation Mark, 7, 60, 175.
Interrogative Sentences, 175, 179.
Inverted Sentences, 177, 178.
Is, Words used after, 149.
Is, are, 15, 16, 21, 80, 83.

Johonnot (Extract), 73.

Keep a Watch on Your Words (Memory Exercise), 71.

Larcom, Lucy (Extract), 63.
Leak in the Dike, The (Phœbe Cary), 142.
Leaves (Composition), 60.
Letters, Omitted, 88.
 Silent, 52.
 Sounds of, 126.
Letter Writing, 92, 93, 99, 101, 102, 106, 117, 120, 130, 140, 141, 146, 155, 156, 165, 168.
Lexington (Holmes), 165.
Like, as, 146.
Lion and the Fox, The (Æsop), 26.
Little Brown Hands (Memory Exercise), 130.
Little People, The (Memory Exercise), 82.
Longfellow, H. W. (Extracts), 76, 123, 124.
Lowell, J. R. (Extract), 107.

Macron, 28.
Mann, Horace (Extract), 106.
May, can, 160.
Me, I, 80.
Memory Exercises, 10, 19, 23, 29, 34, 37, 41, 49, 55, 63, 66, 71, 82, 98, 107, 108, 123, 127, 133, 138, 150, 161, 170, 171.
Merry Christmas (Alcott), 29.
Mispronounced Words, 141, 146.
Misused Words, 121, 146, 147, 160, 162, 165, 166.
Monkey, Cat and Chestnuts, The (Reproduction Exercise), 14.
Monosyllables, 31.
Months, 20, 60, 69.
Most, almost, 147.

Names, 7, 8, 9, 46, 182.
 Common, 61, 183.
 Family, 8.
 Given, 8, 9.
 Proper, 45, 46, 60, 61, 183.
 Special, 61.
Natural Order of Sentences, 177.
Neighborhood Study, 158, 164.
Nobility (Memory Exercise), 150.
Nobody's Child (Phœbe Cary), 133.
Notes for Composition, 153.
Nouns, 61, 182, 183, 188.
 Common, 61, 183.
 Proper, 45, 46, 60, 61, 183.
Number, 61, 63, 74, 75, 84, 135, 182, 186.
Number, Quantity, 166.
Numeral adjectives, 189.

Object, 194.
Odd, strange, funny, 147.
Old Horse's Appeal, The (Reproduction Exercise), 75.
Only, 166.
Opposites, 58.
Our Flag (Conversation Exercise), 38.
Our Own Country (Conversation Exercise), 173.
Ownership, 184.

Paragraphs, 86.
Paul Revere's Ride (Longfellow), 124, 165.
Period, 6, 60, 175.
Person, 186.
Personal Pronouns, 186.
Phrases, 193.
Picture Stories, 12, 16, 20, 24, 32, 39, 43, 47, 57, 62, 70, 81, 85, 101, 118, 154.
Plants, 33, 56.
Plenty, plentiful, 163.
Plural Number, 61, 63, 75, 84, 135, 182, 184, 186.
Poems, Study of, 22, 34, 38, 55, 58, 59, 76, 77, 90, 91, 98, 107, 108, 161, 170, 171.
Poetry, 60, 67.
Polysyllables, 31.
Possessives, 74, 135, 184.
Predicate, 176, 177, 178, 179.
Prefixes, 142, 153.
Prepositions, 194.
Presume, expect, suspect, suppose, 162, 163.
Pronouns, 184, 185, 186, 187, 188.
Pronunciation Exercises, 40, 53, 56, 64, 84, 105, 120, 127.
Proper Adjectives, 189.
Proper Names, or Nouns, 45, 46, 60, 61, 183.
Punctuation, 7, 42, 60, 74, 75, 88, 89, 110, 111, 131, 156, 175, 176, 180, 184.

Quantity, number, 166.
Question Mark, 7, 60, 175.
Questions, 6, 195.
Quotation Marks, 110, 111, 156.
Quotations, Direct, 109, 110, 112, 145, 156.
 Divided, 144.
 Indirect, 110, 111, 112, 145.

Real, very, 121.
Reproduction Exercises, 14, 22, 26, 44, 54, 67, 75, 82, 104, 106, 108, 112, 113, 122, 124, 132, 142, 159.

INDEX. 199

Reviews, 80, 84, 97, 135.
Rhyme, 67.
Robin and Robert (Memory Exercise), 11.
Root Words, 142, 153, 164, 173.

Salt (Information Exercise), 169.
Salutation, 92, 94, 95.
Say No (Composition), 119.
Seeds and Plants (Conversation Exercise), 56.
Sentences, 5, 6, 174, 175.
   Combined, 122, 137, 150.
   Compound, 195, 196.
   Declarative, 175, 179.
   Exclamative, 176.
   Exercise on, 178.
   Imperative, 175, 180, 181.
   Interrogative, 175.
   Inverted, 177, 178, 179.
   Simple, 195, 196.
Seventy-Six (Bryant), 165.
Shall, will, 160.
She, her, 80, 149.
Signature, 96.
Silent Letters, 52.
Simple Subject, 177.
Singular Number, 61, 63, 74, 84, 135, 182, 184, 186.
Snowstorm, The (Composition), 42.
Some, somewhat, 165.
Song, A (Memory Exercise), 23.
Sounds of Consonants, 63.
   of Letters, 126.
Spelling Exercises, 63, 147, 148.
Spiders (Information Exercise), 87.
Squirrel, The (Composition), 72.
Stanzas, 19, 67.
Statements, 5, 6, 195.
   Combined, 122, 137, 150.
Stop, stay, 163.
Strange, odd, funny, 147.
Subject, 176, 177, 178, 179.
Suffixes, 142, 153.
Superscription of Letter, 92.
Surname, 8.
Suspect, suppose, presume, expect, 162, 163.
Syllables, 30, 31.
   Accented, 52.
Synonyms, 116, 117, 136, 148.

Talk about Flies, A (Information Exercise), 50.
Thanksgiving Day (Child), 113.

That, this, these, them, those, 65, 66.
Their, there, 26.
There are, there were, 21.
They, them, 149.
Think, guess, 121.
Thoughts, 174.
Three Bells, The (Whittier), 90.
To, too, two, 25.
To a Waterfowl (Bryant), 171.
Tree, The (Björnson), 37.
Trisyllables, 31.
True Story of a Fishhawk (Reproduction Exercise), 63.
Two, to, too, 25.

Verb Forms, 112, 113, 132, 145, 159, 173.
Verb Phrases, 191.
Verbs, 190, 192.
Verse, 67.
Very, real, 121.
Village Blacksmith, The (Longfellow), 124.
Vowels, 27, 28, 31.
   Sounds of, 48, 49.

Waiting to Grow (Memory Exercise), 34.
Warm Countries (Conversation Exercise), 139.
Was, Words used after, 149.
Was, were, 15, 16, 21, 80, 83.
We, us, 149.
What Robin Told (Memory Exercise), 18.
Whittier, John G. (Extract), 90.
Who, which, 162.
Who, whom, 129.
Will and the Way, The (Memory Exercise), 98.
Willie's First Visit to the Farm (Dictation Exercise), 78.
Will, shall, 160.
Wind and the Leaves, The (Study of Poem), 58.
Wonderful World, The (Memory Exercise), 127, 128.
Wool (Information Exercise), 170.
Words, Derivative, 142, 153, 164, 173.
   Groups of, 193.
   Mispronounced, 141.
   Misused, 121, 146, 147, 160, 162, 165, 166.
   Root, 142, 153, 164, 173.
   Uses of, 174, 181, 182.
Words and their Opposites, 58.
Wreck of the Hesperus, The (Longfellow), 132.

POEMS USED OR REFERRED TO IN THE PRECEDING PAGES.

THESE may be found in the Complete Works of the authors, and in the smaller collections, many of which have been prepared especially for school use.

The teacher is strongly urged to make the reading of the various authors as broad and comprehensive as possible. The lessons in the book are only suggestive of a very extended line of language study, upon the same general plan, in connection with the reading and memorizing of the best productions of standard writers.

The poems of Bryant are published by D. Appleton & Company, 72 Fifth Avenue, New York.

The writings of the Cary Sisters, Holmes, Longfellow, Lowell, and Whittier are published by Houghton, Mifflin & Company, 4 Park Street, Boston, Mass.

The Household Editions of these various authors are published at about $1.50 per vol., postpaid. The smaller collections referred to can be obtained of the publishers named above, postage paid, at from 15 cents to 60 cents each. Among those of special service to teachers are: —

MODERN CLASSICS. — Vol. 1. — LONGFELLOW: Evangeline; The Courtship of Miles Standish; Favorite Poems. Vol. 4. — WHITTIER: Snow Bound; The Tent on the Beach; Favorite Poems. Vol. 5. — LOWELL: The Vision of Sir Launfal; Favorite Poems. Vol. 30. — HOLMES: Favorite Poems; My Hunt after the "Captain."

THE RIVERSIDE LITERATURE SERIES. — No. 1. — Longfellow's Evangeline. No. 4. — Whittier's Snow Bound and Among the Hills. No. 5. — Whittier's Mabel Martin, Maud Muller, and Other Poems. No. 6. — Holmes's Grandmother's Story and Other Poems. No. 11. — Longfellow's The Children's Hour and Other Poems. Nos. 13, 14. — Longfellow's The Song of Hiawatha. No. 30. — Lowell's The Vision of Sir Launfal and Other Pieces. No. 33. — Longfellow's Tales of a Wayside Inn, Part I. No. 38. — Longfellow's The Building of the Ship and Other Poems.

BRYANT LEAFLETS for Homes, Libraries, and Schools.

HOLMES LEAFLETS, containing A Ballad of The Boston Tea Party, Lexington, The Comet, etc.

LONGFELLOW LEAFLETS, containing Paul Revere's Ride, The Building of the Ship, The Children's Hour, and Other Selections.

WHITTIER LEAFLETS, containing Barbara Frietchie, Mabel Martin, Maud Muller, The Three Bells, etc.

Teachers will do well to procure from the various publishers catalogues and lists of special issues of standard works for school use.

www.ingramcontent.com/pod-product-compliance
Lightning Source LLC
Chambersburg PA
CBHW021732220426
43662CB00008B/819